WHEN THE LIES ARE LOUDEST

60 Day Devotional for Fighting Anxiety

By

C. R. Wottrich

Copyright © 2022 Charity Wottrich

All rights reserved. No part of this publication including written material or artwork may be reproduced, distributed, or transmitted in any form or by any means, including photocopying, recording, or other electronic or mechanical methods, without the prior written permission of the author, except in the case of brief quotations embodied in book reviews and certain other noncommercial uses permitted by copyright law.

Scripture quotations are from The ESV® Bible (The Holy Bible, English Standard Version®), copyright © 2001 by Crossway, a publishing ministry of Good News Publishers. Used by permission. All rights reserved.

ISBN: 979-8-9863459-2-5 (Paperback)

First Edition Published 2022

www.CRWottrich.com

CONTENTS

Introduction	1
How to Use This Book	5
DAY 1: God's Word Is Relevant	6
DAY 2: We Deceive Ourselves	9
DAY 3: We Forget Who God Is	12
DAY 4: God's Word Is the Truth	15
DAY 5: We Are Image Bearers	18
DAY 6: Bad Things Happen	21
DAY 7: Sin Has Consequences	24
DAY 8: We Have Hope	27
DAY 9: We Aren't Our Savior	30
DAY 10: Anxiety Is Temporary	33
DAY 11: God Has a Better Plan	36
DAY 12: We Are Gifted Peace	39
DAY 13: We Desire an Escape from Anxiety	42
DAY 14: God Has a Plan for You	45
DAY 15: God's Love Is Steadfast	48
DAY 16: Seek Rejoicing in Suffering	51
DAY 17: God Sustains You	54
DAY 18: Seek Kind Words	57
DAY 19: Seek Contentment	60
DAY 20: Seek Rest	63
DAY 21: Jesus Empathizes	66

DAY 22: Jesus Had Fear	69
DAY 23: Taste and See God's Goodness	72
DAY 24: We Are Adopted	75
DAY 25: Seek God in Distress	78
DAY 26: When Your Emotions Are Tangled	81
DAY 27: Seek Light in Darkness	84
DAY 28: We Have Peace with God	87
DAY 29: We Sometimes Cling to Dust	90
DAY 30: Our Future Is in God's Hands	93
DAY 31: We Have Peace not of this World	96
DAY 32: Fear Is Not God's Gift	99
DAY 33: Don't Fear Judgment	102
DAY 34: Joshua's Commission	105
DAY 35: Cast Your Anxieties on Him	109
DAY 36: Count Others as More Important	112
DAY 37: Carry Others' Burdens	115
DAY 38: Pray for Each Other	118
DAY 39: Boast in Your Weakness	121
DAY 40: Don't Neglect Community	124
DAY 41: God Is in Control	127
DAY 42: The Disciples' Fear	130
DAY 43: Anxiety around Persecution	133
DAY 44: Fearing God	136
DAY 45: Don't Fear, Only Believe	139
DAY 46: Nothing Can Separate Us	142
DAY 47: He Will Sing over You	145

DAY 48: What Can Man Do?	148
DAY 49: God Is with You in the midst of betrayal	151
DAY 50: Peace with Community	154
DAY 51: Sufficient for the Day Is Its Own Trouble	157
DAY 52: Shadow of Death	160
DAY 53: Eye on the Prize	163
DAY 54: Land of Silence	166
DAY 55: Remember What God Has Done	169
DAY 56: Dwelling in Safety	172
DAY 57: God Has a Place for You	175
DAY 58: Remember His Steadfast Love	178
DAY 59: Flooding with Tears	181
DAY 60: Refuge and Strength	184
Closing Comments	187
Resource List	189

INTRODUCTION

Before diving into this devotional, I want to take a moment to express why I am writing this. I have been through a lot of personal hardship. Growing up in a cult, childhood abuse, family difficulties, and the regular life struggles have meshed with my genetic disposition to crown me with clinical anxiety and undiagnosed seasons of depression.

I've wrestled with anxiety for a long time. I don't know when it first began, but it accumulated over time until I could no longer say (as I was apt to), "I'm fine, and I don't need help.".

On the day after Thanksgiving in 2018, I recently moved to Austin from the Northeast states. I was feeling overwhelmed with a new boyfriend, a waitress job that stressed me out to no end, no money to visit anyone for the holidays, and no medical insurance—*that's when it happened*. I was waitressing when I started to feel dizzy and I began experiencing vertigo, head fog, and confusion. I made my way to a manager. *"I feel dizzy,"* was all I could say before she grabbed my arm and helped me sit down—and I did, for what felt like an eternity. I could not shake off the vertigo or other panic attack symptoms. It would not go away, and I was left to conclude that it must be an allergic reaction. Why else would I not be able to make it stop? My boyfriend, now husband, came to drive me to the ER, where I learned it was a panic attack. That incident stopped me from ignoring my mental health and I started taking it seriously. It only took my body shutting down and several thousand dollars in medical debt to do it.

As broke as I was, I spent the following months investing in semi-regular counseling, sparingly using the prescribed meds and stumbling around a lot. One thing I found particularly helpful was my regular Bible reading plan. I started identifying lies I believed about myself and God which fueled my anxiety. I made a list of verses that talked about anxiety or combated the lies I was telling myself. I meditated on these scriptures every morning and prayed over them for a season, and lo and behold it *actually helped*. When I would start to think, *"Everything is out of control, and there's nothing I can do!"* I'd remember that God was in control, and I didn't have to be. When I thought, *"I'm worthless! A failure and fraud!"* I'd remember that I'm made in the image of God (Genesis 1:27), knit together in my mother's womb (Psalm 139:13-14), and known by God. Not only that, but He chose me as one of His adopted children (Ephesians 1:5). The lies I told myself were no match for the truth of scripture.

I found reading about who God is, and who I am in relation to Him very comforting. I also discovered that reading what the Bible says about anxiety and it actually helped decrease the shame I felt. I want to share some of that with you so you can also find peace in God's Word.

I'd like to place a little disclaimer here, the Bible and prayer have not cured me of my anxiety. I have found comfort in God's character and Scripture, but I do not want your goal to be some magical cure. If you suffer from clinical anxiety, consider this book a supplement (not a replacement) to your doctor's recommendations. I also recommend counseling for you if you are anxious or depressed, whether or not you are clinically diagnosed.

God's Word is living and active and profitable for teaching and maturing your faith (Hebrews 4:12, 2 Timothy 3:16-17). Therefore, your anxiety does not have to be something that draws you apart from God. On the contrary, God loves to draw near us, *despite and through* our anxiety.

HOW TO USE THIS BOOK

This devotional book is broken up into 60 sections, one for each day. Pick a time each day that your schedule is not busy, perhaps before work or before you go to sleep at night. Use that time to *be still* and meditate on scripture.

Each day has four sections. First, there is a passage of scripture, followed by some commentary by me, then a section called "Ask Yourself", and ending with "Pray it back to God".

Scripture: At the bare minimum, read the scripture on the page. If you have time, pull out your Bible to read surrounding context and meditate on more scripture.

Commentary: This section is a combination of my personal experience and interpretation of the Word. Use this as a guide for how you should be reading Scripture, but not as flawless truth.

Ask Yourself: This note-taking section is for self reflection. Let scripture stir up your heart and write your answers to the questions.

Pray it back to God: Each day concludes with a guided prayer which draws from the scripture for the day. Use the guided prayer to get started, but don't stop there. Make it personal by praying about people and situations specific to your life.

DAY 1

God's Word Is Relevant

Hebrews 4:12

For the word of God is living and active, sharper than any two-edged sword, piercing to the division of soul and of spirit, of joints and of marrow, and discerning the thoughts and intentions of the heart.

We have to start here. You are about to embark on 60 days of devotions with me, and if you think the Bible is irrelevant to you personally, this book isn't for you. I encourage you to read these scriptures with an open heart. Feel free to meditate on only the passage I share but if you have more time, read the whole chapter for context. I will share a specific scripture that illustrates a narrative about who God is, who we are in our relationship with Him, and how these truths about God should impact how we view our anxiety.

As this passage says, the Word of God is living and active. It discerns the thoughts and intentions of your heart. So, as you read God's word with me, ask yourself: *what is God's Word saying about Himself and me?* God's word is full of life, and I encourage you to treat it that way. As a believer, God's word has the power to bring new life to your soul. It has the power to grow your faith, bring you peace, and revitalize your walk with God. It brings wisdom and guidance into your life that you can't get elsewhere.

Use the Word of God to examine your own heart. God knows your nature better than you know yourself. So, ask yourself the hard questions, and be bold in applying God's word to your life.

Ask yourself:

Am I ready for God's word to speak actively into my life?

_____

_____

_____

Am I prepared for the Bible to pierce my heart and stir up conviction?

_____

_____

_____

Pray it back to God: Dear God, prepare my heart for your word as I continue reading it over the next two months. Help it change me from the inside out. When my heart tells me anything, help me weigh it with your scripture and be convicted. Speak to me in *real-time* through your Word.

DAY 2

We Deceive Ourselves

Jeremiah 17:9

The heart is deceitful above all things, and desperately sick; who can understand it?

In the summer of 2019, I published my memoir about growing up in a cult. Leading up to it's publication, I received a lot of encouragement and support, but I also received some backlash. Someone sent me a 12-page letter telling me why I was wrong and declaring how the sender would treat me if I published the book. I crumpled to the linoleum floor of my kitchen. I couldn't move—I was paralyzed for what felt like a half hour alone in my apartment. I wanted approval from everyone: I wanted to be in control of what people thought about me. I knew I was writing the book for God's glory and not my own, but at that moment, I wanted everyone to *approve of my actions and for me to be in control.*

When I'm in mid-panic, I start thinking about all the things that are wrong or *could* go wrong. The desires of my heart are twisted. I desire approval. I want to be loved, and likewise respected, by the *people* around me. I long to be in control and dwell in safety *by my own doing*. These twisted desires fuel my anxiety and left unchecked, can hurt my spiritual health.

While emotions are not inherently sinful, they often reveal what we love, and we tend to misplace our love (I'm speaking from experience here). For example, I often idolize control and approval, and when these things fade or I *perceive* them as disappearing, I start to panic. Your emotions will tell you where you are placing your love and trust.

Ask yourself:

What are the desires of my heart?

_____

_____

_____

What should my desires be?

_____

_____

_____

Pray it back to God: Lord, your word says my heart is deceitful above all things. Please, help me deny my own desires, which are not based on truth, and help me learn a better way to live. Teach me your desire for me and my life. Help me not to be driven by my emotions.

DAY 3

We Forget Who God Is

Psalm 103:1-5

Bless the Lord, O my soul, and all that is within me, bless his holy name! Bless the Lord, O my soul, and forget not all his benefits, who forgives all your iniquity, who heals all your diseases, who redeems your life from the pit, who crowns you with steadfast love and mercy, who satisfies you with good so that your youth is renewed like the eagle's.

Growing up in a cult has left me believing lies about God. That being said, you don't need a cult to help you come up with wrong ideas about God. You can come up with them on your own just fine. Believing certain things about God that do not line up with scripture might begin seemingly harmless. I used to believe, whether implicitly or explicitly, that I had to *earn my salvation.* That belief bled into my post-cult beliefs, followed me for the next four years, and even to some degree, stayed in the background since I've become a regenerate believer. I sometimes forget that God forgives all iniquity, and He crowns me with steadfast love, so I regularly have to be reminded of God's word.

Another lie I often believe about God is that He can't redeem my life from the pit. I usually try to *do that myself* before asking God to help me. I forget He is my refuge, and I should ask for help. When you find yourself believing lies about God, ask Him for help. As you read through these scriptures, one of my prayers for you is that you would see more clearly who God actually is, and it would cause you to "bless His holy name." As the Psalmist says, let's not forget all His benefits.

Ask yourself:

What do I believe about God's character?

_____

_____

_____

Are there any notions I need to reexamine?

_____

_____

_____

What character traits do I need to be reminded of?

_____

_____

_____

Pray it back to God: Dear Holy God, help me not to forget who you are. Teach me your true character, not just who I imagine you to be. Redeem my life from the pit. Forgive me and help me when I forget your benefits. Remind me of your steadfast love when I forget! Show me your mercy and help me grow in contentment and satisfaction of who you are!

DAY 4

God's Word Is the Truth

2 Timothy 3:16-17

All Scripture is inspired by God and profitable for teaching, for reproof, for correction, for training in righteousness, that the man of God may be complete, equipped for every good work.

You might wonder why I have scripture about the nature of scriptures in a devotional book for someone struggling with anxiety. Well, it's not an accident that I include these passages; you will see more sprinkled throughout this book.

It is important for us to see the value and nature of God's word. If you don't believe it's the inspired Word of God, it's easy to bypass certain sections of scripture or declare that God has nothing to say in His word about your unique situation. That's not true! The Bible is inspired by God and relevant to your life and unique situations. That doesn't mean you will see your name on the page, *"Yo, Charity, you are drinking too much caffeine!"* It doesn't work like that, but it shines a light into our lives, and as you read God's word, I want you to remind yourself that this (not my portion of writing, but the scripture part) is *God's Word*. You can trust it, and it should change you. I'm teaching through it in this book. In some ways, I'm correcting, and in other ways, I'm trying to help train you in righteousness with God's Word.

When you feel anxious and start seeing yourself negatively, telling yourself, *I am not worth it; I am a failure; no one cares about me (fill in your own kind of personal lie)*, you can trust the word of God. The word of God says you are worth it, God succeeded on your behalf, and God cares enough to die for you. The word of God is true, not what you tell yourself when you're anxious—God's word is! It might be hard to believe at the moment, but I'm begging you to cling to that!

Ask yourself:

If all scripture is inspired by God, how should it impact my life?

_____

_____

_____

How can I use God's word to train in righteousness?

_____

_____

_____

How can I use the truth of scripture when I am anxious?

_____

_____

_____

Pray it back to God: Dear God, your word is true. Help me trust that with my whole heart. Give me the wisdom to interpret scripture biblically and not pick and choose what I want to follow. Bring to my mind the truth of scripture when I tell myself lies. I ask you boldly to help me see the value of your Word in a way I have never seen before.

DAY 5

We Are Image Bearers

Genesis 1:27

So God created man in his own image, in the image of God he created him; male and female he created them.

"Everyone hates me," "Something is wrong with me, and I'm beyond help," "I'm going to ruin everything." These statements are lies. If you feel things like this, you're not alone. I've been there myself and I do not think I've heard those lies inside my head for the last time. Those self-devaluing statements are not the truth, but during a panic attack, thoughts like these start finding a foothold in the caverns of my mind.

Suddenly, what the Bible says doesn't matter to me, or at least it fades from my memory. Though I read the Word often and know many truths from scripture, sometimes my wrecked emotions crowd out the truth of God's word and who I am. So, who are we? As humans, we are *made in God's image, designed by Him, intentionally created* by a God of *infinite wisdom and purpose* (See Ephesians 2:10, Genesis 9:6, Colossians 3:10, and Romans 8:29). What does "in God's image" even mean? It means God imparted to us parts of His nature that other creatures do not have. We are a reflection (or image) of some of God's nature.

God has gifted us with self-awareness and the ability to create. We are intelligent creatures with logic and reasoning, a desire for community, and we have authority and stewardship over the earth, to name a few characteristics of God that we share. We were also gifted with emotions in a way that animals don't have. You have value apart from anything you do or don't do, despite how you look or who your earthly family is. You are a beautiful creation of the maker of all things. You are made in God's image, which is enough to give you *value and purpose*.

Ask yourself:

How often do I remind myself that I was created by God in His image?

_____

_____

_____

Where do I place my value?

_____

_____

_____

In what ways do I reflect the image of God, and in what ways do I not?

_____

_____

_____

Pray it back to God: Dear God, the Word says you created me in your image. I have inherent value as a human being because you designed me, and I'm a reflection (if only in small ways) of parts of your nature. Help me place my value in that, not success or failure, relationships, career, finances, emotional state, physical health, or any other earthly picture of value. I want to constantly be reminded that I am an image bearer of your glory, created by you. Please, help me remember that.

DAY 6

Bad Things Happen

Romans 5:12

Therefore, just as through one man sin entered into the world, and death through sin, and so death spread to all men, because all sinned—

We were made in the image of God (Genesis 1:27), but that image was corrupted by the fall of mankind. Not only was sin and death something that corrupted and continues to corrupt the world around us, but it also wreaks havoc inside us.

Our nature is not pure; just as disease comes with sin, so do misfortunes and *mental illness*. Sin has consequences. Often, they are small earthly consequences, but sometimes they are devastatingly large consequences. With the first sin came inherited consequences. The beautiful garden that Adam and Eve lived in—a beautiful picture of God's design—has faded away, and in its place, we are left with death and all the decay that comes with it. This is a harsh consequence and a hard devotional to go through if you don't know that *there is hope*.

This world is not our ultimate home; we are not promised sunshine and roses every day. Instead, we are promised a future hope and for God to be with us. So, until heaven, we will have to live in a world where sin and death wreak havoc, where the personal consequences of sin cause decay in our lives and others, and the overarching implications of sin impact our lives in devastating ways.

Along with everything that the fall impacted, it also effected our emotions. Emotions aren't inherently bad. They are beautiful in the context of God's perfect plan, but they are lacking in our current fallen condition. We desire things not according to God's plan, and when we don't feel secure in obtaining or retaining that thing, we get anxious. We can also become anxious or depressed because godly desires are being disrupted, but that heartache and heartbreak are not pictures of Eden. It's our response to a broken world.

Ask yourself:

How is my anxiety a reflection of the fall?

_____

_____

_____

What ideals do I long for?

_____

_____

_____

Which of my desires long for a perfect Eden or seek pleasure or purpose in something not of God?

_____

_____

_____

Pray it back to God: Dear God, reading about the fall can be so disheartening. Help me process it in a healthy way. Help me recognize this world has fallen while clinging to you as my hope. Be my guide in handling my mental state, which is imperfect because of the fall. Help me desire the right things and be with me while I struggle with my mental health.

DAY 7

Sin Has Consequences

Psalm 39:6-13

Surely a man goes about as a shadow! Surely for nothing they are in turmoil; man heaps up wealth and does not know who will gather! "And now, O Lord, for what do I wait? My hope is in you. Deliver me from all my transgressions. Do not make me the scorn of the fool! I am mute; I do not open my mouth, for it is you who have done it. Remove your stroke from me; I am spent by the hostility of your hand. When you discipline a man with rebukes for sin, you consume like a moth what is dear to him; surely all mankind is a mere breath! Selah "Hear my prayer, O Lord, and give ear to my cry; hold not your peace at my tears! For I am a sojourner with you, a guest, like all my fathers. Look away from me, that I may smile again, before I depart and am no more!"

As saved sons and daughters of God, we don't have to worry about eternal punishment, but our actions have very real consequences. Everything we do matters, and when we sin, it can cause a ripple effect of hurt relationships, destructive habits, loss of jobs, or other hardships brought on by our sins. If your anxiety is related to sins you have committed, you don't need to walk through that alone. God paid the penalty for your sin, so you don't have to hold on to guilt and shame forever.

I can't say which sufferings are a consequence of your sin and what things are simply a consequence of the fall, but what I can say is that *either way,* you need to take it all to Jesus. Ask Him for grace and mercy, for He is a gracious God, slow to anger and abounding in steadfast love.

Ask yourself:

What hardship have I suffered because of the fall?

_____

_____

What hardships have I suffered as a consequence of my own sin?

_____

_____

How can I lean on God amidst this brokenness?

_____

_____

Pray it back to God: Dear God, I know my actions have consequences. Lord, I can't fight my bad habits alone. I am incapable of doing anything good without the help of the Holy Spirit. Please, be merciful to me, a sinner. Help me grow from my mistakes and be quick to repent and change. Redeem all the broken parts of my story and save me from the messes I create. Save me for the sake of your steadfast love, even though I don't deserve it. Help me not fear my sin or the consequences. Instead, help me depend on you and your mercy to see me through to the other side.

DAY 8

We Have Hope

Romans 5:18-19

Therefore, as one trespass led to condemnation for all men, so one act of righteousness leads to justification and life for all men. For as by the one man's disobedience the many were made sinners, so by the one man's obedience the many will be made righteous.

We know this is a fallen world, but to leave it there would be a mistake. Reading about how this world was corrupted by sin and death (while necessary) can be heartbreaking. We must not despair, though, for we are loved and not forgotten. After the fall, God had the option and right to leave sin and death to wreak havoc on the earth until the end of time. He had the right to condemn us to eternal punishment for our own personal sins.

Praise God that is not the end of the story! Just as one man brought sin and death into the world by an act of disobedience, so one man (y'all know Him as Jesus) brought life, hope, and redemption through His act of love and obedience on the cross. He bore our sin, paid our debt for sin by dying in our place, while also CONQUERING death by His resurrection on the third day! Writing these words is encouraging to me today. Even though I only started writing the first draft of this book a few days ago, I have already fallen behind some goals I'd set for myself. I feel a little inner despair at how I've fallen short so soon into my goals.

As I'm writing this, yesterday was Easter Sunday. Why am I so quick to forget Easter and everything that it represents? Jesus died for our sins and conquered death so that we can have an eternity with Him as righteous children of God. He took our sin and made us clean. Because of Jesus, there is hope. We can count on His love and presence in our lives now and in our eternal home.

I urge you to look back on your own personal salvation, when you found this hope for the first time. How did that make you feel? How did Jesus change you?

Ask yourself:

Am I regularly reminded of my hope in Christ and God's love for me?

___

___

___

If so, how would my life change?

___

___

___

Jesus conquered death and started the reversal of the fall; what does that mean for my mental health struggle?

___

___

___

Pray it back to God: Dear God, you are my hope and salvation. This world was broken by us, and no matter how we try to piece it together, without you, our efforts fall short. I need you to remind me daily that you are my hope because I often forget. Remind me I am loved and not alone in my struggle. Be with me. Thank you for conquering sin and death. Help me look to you for my hope.

DAY 9

We Aren't Our Savior

Ephesians 2:8-9

For by grace you have been saved through faith. And this is not your own doing; it is the gift of God, not a result of works, so that no one may boast.

"I'm a failure." "I am not enough." "God couldn't love someone like me." Be encouraged that you are not alone if you ever have feelings like these. There is an aspect of these statements that actually is true, but it's not the whole truth. These feelings say, *"There is something lacking in my actions; I fall short,"* and that statement is true; we do fall short. The truth is, though, we don't have to succeed in everything because Jesus made a way for us. While we should strive to obey God's law, grow in discipline, and fight sin, we should not despair when we fail or feel like we are not enough. Jesus *was and is* enough so that we don't have to be. He didn't need us, and we couldn't measure up, but He CHOSE and SAVED us because He LOVES us.

It's as the text says; it's not anything we have done but purely because God changed our hearts and gave us our salvation. That's the truth. It's easy for me to get it twisted sometimes and think it depends on what I do, but it doesn't. So, the next time you feel like a failure or unworthy of love, please remind yourself that it's not about what standard you can stick to, but because *God chose you*. You don't have to despair! Don't let your accomplishments or failures dictate your attitude about yourself. This should make you humble and full of gratitude.

Ask yourself:

Am I humble and full of gratitude for what God's done for me?

_____

_____

_____

Do I look at my actions as a measurement of my worth or lack thereof?

_____

_____

_____

Pray it back to God: Dear God, thank you for saving me. Thank you for choosing to save me amid my sins, failures, and shortcomings. I miss the mark so much and sometimes put my value there. Please, remind me that my value is not found in what I do but in *what you did for me.*

DAY 10

Anxiety Is Temporary

Revelation 21:4

"He will wipe away every tear from their eyes, and death shall be no more, neither shall there be mourning, nor crying, nor pain anymore, for the former things have passed away."

While emotions are good, mental illness and heartache are not the realizations of God's perfect plan. Mental illness is temporary. Perhaps for a season, and maybe for the rest of your life here on earth. However, when you see Jesus face to face, there will be no more sad tears and hidden despair. On that day, there will be joy. For now, we can seek comfort and peace from our Heavenly Father, but later, we will see Him clearly, and there will be *no more pain.*

In hoping and meditating on this future, I have tears in my eyes right now. Oh, *how I long* for my anxiety to be gone forever, and when it is, I don't know what my eyes will do if happy tears aren't a thing (I think they will be). While we toil for a little while, we will have eternity in paradise. My mind can't picture it! How can my anxiety just be *gone*? What will it feel like to have no more worries and emotional pain? To have no more restless nights turning and trying to fall asleep, no more night terrors, no more panic attacks at the grocery store, no more laying on the shower floor in despair. *No more pain.*

Right before Jesus died on the cross for our sins, He said, *"It is finished."* His death was sufficient to pay our penalty for sin and make a way for eternity with God in paradise. So, while we will still suffer from our own sinful nature and the effects of mental illness in this life, that is so temporary compared to how long eternity is. God has a plan for us here on this earth, and when He has fulfilled that plan in us, He will take us home. Praise God for that reality that we can hold on to! The comfort we find in Him now, amid our struggles, is just a taste of that future comfort.

Ask yourself:

Have I considered the impermanence of my mental illness or struggle?

_____

_____

_____

How does meditating on that future day make me feel?

_____

_____

_____

Why should I turn to God for comfort?

_____

_____

_____

Pray it back to God: Dear God, you are the king of comfort. You died, so that sin and death do not own us. I long to be forever free of the effects of mental illness. Give me the vision to picture that day and find hope in knowing that pain does not last forever. Meanwhile, be with me amidst my current struggles. Help me know your presence and comfort in a tangible way.

DAY 11

God Has a Better Plan

Proverbs 16:9

The heart of man plans his way, but the Lord establishes his steps.

I've got a rigid plan for writing this because I need structure to stay on track. I'm kind of a perfectionist and procrastinator with mood swings, and writing is not a walk in the park. Don't get me wrong, writing is very fulfilling to me, but at this moment, as I'm off to a late start, I feel so much guilt and shame. I know the plans are vital for me to stay on track, but I'm placing that importance at such a level that missing the mark, *even just a little,* is giving me anxiety. I opened up my outline today and saw this verse staring me in the face.

Let me remind you; I'm not writing this devotional book because I'm an expert at not being anxious; *far* from that. I'm writing this because the Word of God has a way of interrupting my life and anxieties with truth. This morning is one of those moments. I don't feel all better, but I feel more at peace. I have a plan to stick to today that I created, but if life gets in the way and it doesn't happen quite the way I imagined, that's a-okay.

The heavens won't fall; I'm not a failure. I'm not less genuine, and my identity is not shaken.

I want you to think about your plans for your life, the things that have gone wrong in the past, and the things you worry about going wrong in the future. We can plan, but as the verse says, the Lord establishes our steps. We may envision entering our sophomore year in the coming year, getting married, having a kid, or writing a book. I think making plans and expectations for your future is natural and good, but the more open-handedly we hold that plan, the better. I don't mean you shouldn't have resolve, discipline, or wait for signs in the skies to decide, but sometimes the boat will get rocked. At other times, you will have to drop out of school, break up with your boyfriend, have infertility issues, and get your book writing plans interrupted. It's happened many times to me, and sometimes, those interruptions are welcomed and good. Occasionally, those interruptions are painful, but it will be okay. God is sovereign over our path. As much as we like to imagine we are in control, it will become more apparent that is not the case as life goes on. The question is, do you trust God's plan?

Ask yourself:

What ways have my plans been interrupted in the past?

_____

_____

_____

Do I hold my future plans with open hands?

_____

_____

_____

Do I trust God's plan for my life?

_____

_____

_____

Pray it back to God: Dear God, I have a vision for my life. I have hopes and dreams that I *really* want to happen. Help me not be anxious about my future or depressed about my past. Help me not to fixate on the what-ifs of my life. I know you are the one who establishes my steps. Help me trust that you have the perfect plan for my life.

DAY 12

We Are Gifted Peace

Philippians 4:7

And the peace of God, which surpasses all understanding, will guard your hearts and your minds in Christ Jesus.

One of my closest friends recently said to me that when talking about anxiety that she thought I had so much peace. Here is someone very familiar with my anxiety, yet she's saying I have peace? Because I have *so much* anxiety, I don't think of myself as someone who has peace. How can I be *an anxious person* and also be a peaceful person? The truth is, I'm not "an anxious person;" I am "a person who struggles with anxiety." I sometimes get those things mixed up, and my anxiety feels like a part of my *very identity*. It is not part of my identity, though, and I'm here to remind you that your anxiety is likewise not part of yours.

Yes, I'm anxious often, but I also have peace. I have someone to turn to, and I often find myself thinking, *"How am I not having a panic attack right now?" "Why is this news not absolutely flooring me?" "How is it I'm taking that constructive criticism and not being consumed with feelings of failure?" "How is it I'm ready to take this leap of faith despite the potential pitfalls along the way?"* God's peace is present in my life.

One of the ways I've experienced God's peace was soon after I'd moved to Austin, Texas. I was 20, new to a city with no real friends yet, over 1000 miles from most of my immediate family, and keenly aware that 90% of my 13 siblings, their spouses, and my parents disapproved of my decisions and plans. Yup, if there was a time for despair, self-deprecating thoughts, and anxiety to settle, it would be then, and settle it did. Amidst overwhelming and tearful days, I realized I was not fully alone. With nowhere to turn but up, God filled the void I was feeling. I turned to Him regularly, and He was there for me every time I did. I experienced more dependence on God than ever before. All I had to do was ask, and I felt His presence.

I've also experienced God's peace over time. As I've continued to stay in God's word, prayer, and community, I've noticed that although my anxiety is still present, there is a low level of background peace that regularly combats my anxiety. I'm still getting the attacks, but I have better shields up and finer counter-attacks.

Ask yourself:

When last did I experience the gift of God's peace?

_____

_____

_____

Do I regularly ask for God's peace?

_____

_____

_____

What is stopping me from stepping out in faith and making a habit of seeking God's peace?

_____

_____

_____

Pray it back to God: Dear God, when I am anxious, help me not to stay afraid. Help me find peace. You have a peace that transcends understanding, and I want that peace in my life. I want it every day and in every stressful situation. Help me rely on you despite and through my anxiety. Bring me your peace!

DAY 13

We Desire an Escape from Anxiety

Psalm 55:4-8 & 16-18

My heart is in anguish within me; the terrors of death have fallen upon me. Fear and trembling come upon me, and horror overwhelms me. And I say, "Oh, that I had wings like a dove! I would fly away and be at rest; yes, I would wander far away; I would lodge in the wilderness; Selah. I would hurry to find a shelter from the raging wind and tempest. (…) But I call to God, and the Lord will save me. Evening and morning and at noon I utter my complaint and moan, and he hears my voice. He redeems my soul in safety from the battle that I wage, for many are arrayed against me.

This passage from the Psalms has been of great comfort to me. I often feel those same emotions when I am anxious or depressed. I just want to get away, be carefree, and forget all my troubles. This is not what God has for us. There is no magic cure to anxiety; although God has miraculous power to heal mental illness like every other disease, that is not always His plan (at least, not while we are on earth). So, when we find ourselves under the oppression of mental illness, we should turn to Him.

I want to fly away with my wings. I want to escape, and I want to do that my way. On different days, that phrase means different things. One of those things is watching sitcoms; I'm addicted to watching sitcoms as an escape mechanism. It started when I was under 18, still under my parents' roof and subsequent authority. I was coerced into attending the Branhamism church for about six months after I stopped believing it. Many sermons would preach against people like me, who did not believe what they believed. It was about how we were damned and how people shouldn't be friends with us. I felt alone and scared. I wasn't sure my friends were real, and I had too many troubles to count. So, I turned to a screen to escape my reality. I had real fear and depression. I needed counseling, possibly medication, and I definitely needed God. Instead of turning to Him, however, I constructed some wings of my own and flew away.

Later, my more harmful escape was a pornography addiction that plagued me for several years. Even if what you turn to is cardio or schoolwork, supposedly "not so bad" or "good things," there is no substitute for praying and turning to God for comfort. He will save and sustain you. It's not a one-and-done thing either; turn to Him often. Maybe it won't be "every morning, noon, and night" like the Psalm describes, but please, schedule a regular time to turn to God because He hears you.

Ask yourself:

Do I wish I had the power to escape my circumstances? Do I wish I could rescue myself or look to God for help?

_____

_____

_____

What is my version of "flying away"?

_____

_____

_____

How is turning to God better than 'flying away'?

_____

_____

_____

Pray it back to God: Dear God, sometimes, I wish I had wings and could just fly away from it all. I sometimes wish I could just escape all that life throws at me, but I turn to you instead. You see my tears and hear my prayers. My inner turmoil is not a surprise to you. Bring my heart back to safety, be with me, and comfort me. Be my protection.

DAY 14

God Has a Plan for You

Ephesians 2:10

For we are his workmanship, created in Christ Jesus for good works, which God prepared beforehand, that we should walk in them.

Anxiety can sometimes leave you feeling like you need to have the perfect plan or know your purpose right away to create a life of value. This is not true! I know sometimes it can feel this way, and those feelings are real, but the statement behind those feelings is a lie. I encourage you to lean on this scripture truth when you feel like there is no plan for you. Even if you don't think your giftings are worthwhile, the Bible says differently. You are God's workmanship; He created you and doesn't make mistakes! With the help of Jesus, you will be able to glorify God with your life.

If you have no idea how to do that, don't despair. God has a wonderful way of turning things around and using even the unplanned or mundane things for His glory. For now, take it one step at a time. If you see something you feel called in, whether pursuing scripture, praying more, or taking that job offer and working with integrity—walk in the way set before you. Even if you can't find a particular thing right now, continue to walk with Him. Don't let your time with God cease when this devotional book ends. Pick a Bible reading plan and stick to it. Pray over the text like we've been doing in this book. Take it one day at a time and continue to thank God for how you see Him moving in your life. Continue to ask Him what He has prepared for you to do.

Ask yourself

Do I believe God has a plan for me?

_____

_____

_____

How could God be using my current situation for His glory?

_____

_____

_____

Are there things I see I should be walking in?

_____

_____

_____

Pray it back to God: Dear God, thank you for preparing a plan for me. Thank you for creating me with purpose. Thank you for using me, weak as I am, for your glory. I don't know all your plans for me, but I pray you would guide me in walking in them. Help me find fulfillment and satisfaction in my current situation. Help me always to stay humble and lean on you for my strength to keep walking.

DAY 15

God's Love Is Steadfast

Psalm 118:1-6

Oh give thanks to the Lord, for he is good; for his steadfast love endures forever! Let Israel say, "His steadfast love endures forever." Let the house of Aaron say, "His steadfast love endures forever." Let those who fear the Lord say, "His steadfast love endures forever." Out of my distress I called on the Lord; the Lord answered me and set me free. The Lord is on my side; I will not fear.

"Steadfast love" is a concept that has been increasingly comforting to me as I see that phrase throughout the Old Testament, and especially in the Book of Psalms. Merriam-Webster dictionary defines 'steadfast' as "firmly fixed in place: IMMOVABLE" and "not subject to change." This is the way God's love is described. It's immovable, fixed, never changing, always there, no matter what you do or don't do, whether you are feeling it or not. It's still there.

When you feel unloved or unlovable, I want you to remember not only what Jesus did on the cross for you because He loves you, but also the truth of scripture. God's love is steadfast; it endures forever. So, call to the Lord in your distress, and He will set you free. Call to Him and feel His steadfast love surround you.

This verse also mentions 'fearing God'. This can be a deep one, but I'll boil it down for us today. Essentially, fearing God means placing Him as your biggest priority and acknowledging Him as *the* biggest authority. Fearing God above your anxiety means believing He is greater than it. One tangible example would be that scripture has the final say when held up to the words of our mental illness. This means that part of growing in fearing God should naturally help you rely on Him more than your sinful nature or emotions.

Ask yourself:

Do I have trouble seeing God's love as 'steadfast'?

_____

_____

_____

Do I fear the Lord more than I fear my anxiety?

_____

_____

_____

Pray it back to God: Dear God, please be with me. Show me your steadfast love; make it apparent to me now and often. I want to feel your love every hour of every day. I know it's there, but sometimes, I forget. Help me also to fear you above my mental struggles. My struggle is real, but you and your power are greater. Amid my distress, help me remember that.

DAY 16

Seek Rejoicing in Suffering

Romans 5:3-5

Not only that, but we rejoice in our sufferings, knowing that suffering produces endurance, and endurance produces character, and character produces hope, and hope does not put us to shame, because God's love has been poured into our hearts through the Holy Spirit who has been given to us.

Rejoicing in suffering seems very mysterious to me. Yet, it's one of those paradoxical things we are called to believe as followers of Christ. So, what does it practically, *tangibly* look like to rejoice when you are suffering? First, I'll tell you what it doesn't mean. It doesn't mean being thankful for losing your job, being happy about the disunity in your family, enjoying the mental anguish after a grievous sin, or feeling totally pumped when someone persecutes you for being a Christian or speaking the truth.

It does mean having a joy not dependent on your situation. For example, Paul and Silas sang songs of praise to God in prison. Talk about not finding your joy in your circumstances (James

1:2-18) They worshiped God despite and through immense suffering.

As this passage says, we can rejoice in suffering by being reassured that this suffering is not meaningless. God has a purpose even for this situation. It will build character, endurance, and hope. When we rejoice and have hope amid our suffering, our hope will not put us to shame. Unlike our anxiety telling us ugly lies about our situation, who we are, and who God is, hope tells us the beautiful truth that there is something to rejoice about: a power higher than us who has helped us and will continue to help us.

The Holy Spirit within us will help us find hope. Even though we suffer, God will always be with you and love you. You've been saved by His blood and through His great love, and no situation or emotion can take that away from you. So, I'd say that's something to rejoice about.

Ask yourself:

When was the last time I rejoiced amid suffering?

_____

_____

_____

How did that impact my situation in the moment, and after the fact?

_____

_____

_____

Can I process my painful emotions while simultaneously having hope?

_____

_____

_____

Pray it back to God: Dear God, my mental illness can make any suffering amplified. Help me find genuine joy in the midst of and despite my suffering. Help me have hope and peace that transcends understanding. Help me see that you are with me and worthy of worship and praise, even though my current situation looks so bleak. I praise you, God! Thank you for being with me and making a way for me to be with you in eternity.

DAY 17

God Sustains You

Psalm 3:3-5

But you, O Lord, are a shield about me, my glory, and the lifter of my head. I cried aloud to the Lord, and he answered me from his holy hill. Selah

I lay down and slept; I woke again, for the Lord sustained me.

This psalm has been of so much comfort to me amid painful anxiety. I have the words "He answered me" and "I awoke again" underlined in my Bible. If you read the whole chapter, you will see that David is very aware of his enemies around him. They are even described as saying, "There is no salvation for him in God", and yet, David declares that he will not be afraid of the many thousands of people, he declares truths of scripture on what He knows about God and His promises.

I just love that. I love how David's prayers and humble psalms like this one are a part of our holy scriptures. When I received pushback from many people about my memoir, *Where the Willow Weeps*, I had to keep reminding myself of God's promises. People who were a part of Branhamism were saying things like, *"There is no salvation for her in God"*, or *"God will punish you for this"*. or *"You're a demon."* Although I knew those things weren't true, they still affected me. It still made me fearful of these people and what other hurtful things they might do or say.

When I was fearful and didn't know how to make it to the other side of writing my book, I would see this passage and remember who it is that protects and sustains me. I knew that even if I cried myself to sleep, it would be a new day when I woke up. I could count on God to be with me through the writing of that book. Also, I know you can count on Him to sustain you and walk with you through whatever trial you are experiencing right now. Whether it's a specific situation or your ongoing anxiety, God will lift your head, hear you, and sustain you until the next day.

Ask yourself:

Do I look to God to sustain me?

_____

_____

_____

When's the last time I thanked God for the simple things like helping me lift my head off my pillow in the morning?

_____

_____

_____

Pray it back to God: Dear God, you have willed every moment I live in this life. You are the creator of my life and sustainer of my very breath. Lord, I pray that you stay with me in the little things, like trying to fall asleep at night and waking up in the morning. Make your presence known and help me be filled with gratitude for simple moments like those. Thank you, dear God, for sustaining and bringing me through each trial. Help me make it to the other side.

DAY 18

Seek Kind Words

Proverbs 12:25

Anxiety in a man's heart weighs him down, but a good word makes him glad.

We should seek to show other people the same kind words we want to be greeted with and encouraged by. Think about the last time you were having a very anxious day, and someone went out of their way to say something nice to you. I kind of text in the middle of an anxious day saying, "Hey, thanks for being such a good friend!", "I saw this post, and I thought of you," or "I'm praying for you today! You've got this friend." All these mean so much to me. When I'm anxious and hear something like that, tears fill my eyes (yes, I'm a bit of a crier). I thank God for that little ray of hope on what otherwise felt like a hopeless day.

Another vital part of seeking kind words is surrounding yourself with encouraging people. Don't get me wrong, I don't just mean people pleasers who love to flatter you (oh no, no, no), but I mean Spirit-filled, kind-hearted people who will encourage you in the faith. People who will not only challenge you and call out sin when it is appropriate, but who will also pray for you and read the Bible with you. You need people in your life who are full of grace and kindness in their speech.

By saying we need to seek kind words, I mean more than surrounding ourselves with encouraging people and showing kindness to others: but also we should seek to speak kind words to ourselves.

Personally, I think I'm pretty good at encouraging others, but I struggle to treat myself with the same love. I struggle with many self-esteem issues, which means my anxiety sometimes tells me all kinds of lies about who I am or discourages me from doing important things. When we are in moments like that, we need to remember who we are and speak good words over ourselves.

Ask yourself:

Do I speak kind words to others?

_____

_____

_____

Do I have people in my life who encourage me when I am anxious?

_____

_____

_____

Do I show the same kindness to myself as I show others: the type of kindness laid out in scripture?

_____

_____

_____

Pray it back to God: Dear God, help me seek kind words. Help me be an encouragement to other people who are fighting struggles—whatever they are struggling with—and help me be kind to myself. Help me internalize the truth of who I am as is laid out in scripture.

DAY 19

Seek Contentment

Hebrews 13:5-6

Keep your life free from love of money, and be content with what you have, for he has said, "I will never leave you nor forsake you." So we can confidently say, "The Lord is my helper; I will not fear; what can man do to me?"

The love of money doesn't just mean greed. It doesn't just mean things like accepting an unethical job offer because the salary is good. It doesn't just mean avoiding a call to go to the nations because you don't want to give up your comfortable job or home. The love of money can look like discontentment and sitting in anxiety related to money. For example, I often daydream about things I want to buy. For me, that might mean some trendy home decor or new clothes, but for you, it might mean dreaming about your fantasy home, wide flat screen TV, new gadget, or fancy event. It's okay to dream, but we need to hold our desires with an open hand.

What about anxiety related to money problems? How can that be greed? Well, the anxiety might not be greed, but it shows the desires of your heart. Anxiety can be a tool to see our hearts' idols, and being anxious about money might mean you've got a lot of love for money in your heart.

When you are anxious about money, take the opportunity to trust in God. We should say, as the author of Hebrews says (quoting the Psalms), *"The Lord is my helper; I will not fear; what can man do to me?"* Something that helped me in the most broke time of my life was saying, *"What is the worst thing that could happen?"* This might seem counterintuitive for stalling your anxiety but hear me out. The worst (reasonable thing) that could happen was usually me going deeper in debt, missing rent, getting kicked out, and having to trespass on friends' hospitality while I found better work. Don't get me wrong, my worst-case scenario was terrifying to me, and maybe yours is worse and scarier, but when I followed my anxious thoughts to their farthest thought, I would see that it still wasn't *that* bad. My salvation would still be secure; I'd still be a child of God, loved, and I would never be truly alone. Remember that no matter how dire your financial circumstance is, the most important thing is not the number in your bank account or student loan bill.

Ask yourself:

How do my finances affect my anxiety?

_____

_____

_____

Do I sometimes fall into a love of money?

_____

_____

_____

How can I grow in finding contentment in God?

_____

_____

_____

Pray it back to God: Dear God, I am sometimes anxious about my finances. I know that this indicates a love of money in me. Help me love and trust you more than I find security in my financial state. I also pray that I'd keep my identity firmly planted as your child and not in what I wear, eat, or live. Help me grow in contentment.

DAY 20

Seek Rest

Matthew 11:28-30

"Come to me, all who labor and are heavy laden, and I will give you rest. Take my yoke upon you, and learn from me, for I am gentle and lowly in heart, and you will find rest for your souls. For my yoke is easy, and my burden is light."

Jesus Christ has eternally existed as God, together with the Father and the Spirit, but when Jesus was made man, He was limited in some ways. This is difficult to comprehend because Jesus, being fully God, had the power to heal the sick and raise the dead, but by willingly taking on human flesh, He submitted Himself to the human condition, growing physically tired, sleepy, and hungry. Jesus humbled Himself to fulfill the scriptures, by taking on weakness, He was able to be pierced for our transgression and crushed for our iniquity (Isaiah 53:5). He chose to be temporarily limited in some capacity with things like *His time*. I think it's amazing that at the time Jesus was initially saying this, He was speaking to those around Him, inviting people to come to Him for rest while He also needed rest, weary from fasting, and traveling on foot from town to town.

If Jesus could find time for the crowds that came to Him while He was in the flesh here on earth, how much more can He who is above the heavens, unbound by time, bring rest to our weary souls? He is gentle and humble and will never turn one of His children away.

Ask yourself:

Where do I primarily go for rest?

_____

_____

_____

Do I find a satisfying rest in those things?

_____

_____

_____

What keeps me from turning to Jesus when I am weary and heavy-laden?

_____

_____

_____

Pray it back to God: Dear God, you humbled yourself and became human. You lived the life we never could, and in doing so, you paid our debts. Thank you for that. I also thank you for the rest that is found in your presence. Help me come to you often; remind me of my need for you and the hollowness of other forms of escape that I often seek instead of you.

DAY 21

Jesus Empathizes

Hebrews 4:14-16

Since then we have a great high priest who has passed through the heavens, Jesus, the Son of God, let us hold fast our confession. For we do not have a high priest who is unable to sympathize with our weaknesses, but one who in every respect has been tempted as we are, yet without sin. Let us then with confidence draw near to the throne of grace, that we may receive mercy and find grace to help in time of need.

If you are guilty of thinking to yourself, "no one understands me," or "no one sees me." you'd be wrong. The scripture says Jesus can empathize with us, having suffered much and tempted as we are. The difference between the life Jesus lived and our life is that despite suffering and temptation, Jesus always held fast to the truth and avoided sin.

Jesus experienced poverty, He got physically tired, He experienced grief, and He knows what it feels like to be betrayed and tried unjustly. Jesus had a fear of the future, experienced great emotional anguish in the garden of Gethsemane, and even knows what it's like to feel forsaken by God. It's easy to think of God as a faraway force instead of an all-knowing, and yes, even *empathetic* God. Yet, that's true! We not only have an advocate in God (if that wasn't enough already), but His compassion and comfort really do come from a place of true understanding.

As a woman who grew up in a cult where women were ostracized, abused, and silenced, it's hard to see how Jesus can relate to me. I have experienced sexual harassment in the workplace and childhood molestation. I've had night terrors caused by past trauma, and as someone who's experienced a secret addiction to pornography, I find it difficult to see how the Lord feels my pain. I know He experienced great suffering, much of which exceeds mine. I know He also experienced many temptations, which were probably even greater than mine, because He actually kept fighting it to the end instead of giving in. Despite all this, I feel like my story is too unique for Him to relate to. That feeling is valid, but it's not based on reality. If the Bible says Jesus can empathize with us, then that's what I choose to believe.

There is no long-term comfort for me to hold on to my *feeling* that God does not understand. Yet, there is much long-lasting comfort in knowing that God understands what I'm going through, both because of His omniscience (the fact that He literally knows everything) and because He lived a hard life, too.

Ask yourself:

When I pray, do I assume God can understand, or do I come to Him thinking He does not?

_____

_____

_____

How should the fact that Jesus empathizes with my life change how I pray?

_____

_____

_____

What is the benefit of God being able to relate to my suffering?

_____

_____

_____

Pray it back to God: Dear God, I sometimes feel like I'm all alone in my experience and that no one gets what I've been through. Thank you for coming to this world as a man and walking in our shoes. Thank you for living perfectly and taking our punishment upon yourself. Help me remember that you too, were tempted and suffered when I feel alone.

DAY 22

Jesus Had Fear

Mark 14:32-26

And they went to a place called Gethsemane. And he said to his disciples, "Sit here while I pray." And he took with him Peter and James and John, and began to be greatly distressed and troubled. And he said to them, "My soul is very sorrowful, even to death. Remain here and watch." And going a little farther, he fell on the ground and prayed that, if it were possible, the hour might pass from him. And he said, "Abba, Father, all things are possible for you. Remove this cup from me. Yet not what I will, but what you will."

I share this passage for two reasons: one is that if Jesus felt sorrowful even unto death, we should not feel ashamed of feeling those emotions, even if the reasons we are feeling those emotions don't seem to justify the feeling. Jesus was perfect— He lived a life without sin; therefore, strong negative emotions are not inherently sinful (even if our desires or reason might be). While our emotions might sometimes point out things we value too much, they are not inherently sinful. Therefore, you should not berate yourself for feeling anxiety—we live in a broken world, and fear and grief exist to help us deal with that.

Sometimes, that fear and grief grow out of proportion and can become a problem in itself. However, negative emotions are not sinful responses to the brokenness and suffering happening in a fallen world.

The second reason is that I think Jesus models beautifully what we should do with our anxiety or other emotional weight. We should share those feelings with our community, AND most importantly, share those fears with our Heavenly Father in prayer. When we feel the pain of anxiety, it's easy to turn inward to look for strength out of our own willpower and grit or turn to something external that numbs or distracts us from that fear. Unfortunately, these ways of coping with anxiety often make us lose control over our emotions, and we feel ashamed at being unable to keep them in check. In another way, they can turn into bad habits. I'm not saying all coping mechanisms are harmful. I am saying no coping mechanism, determination, discipline, and yes, no medicine should replace sharing with your community and trusting God in prayer. Sometimes, good coping mechanisms or healthy habit changes will lessen our anxiety.

Ask yourself:

Do I view my anxiety as a stain on my character or something I am ashamed of?

_____

_____

_____

How should the fact that Jesus experienced fear and grief change how I view my own? What can I learn from Jesus's response to His own emotions?

_____

_____

_____

Pray it back to God: Dear God, I sometimes feel weighed down by my negative emotions. Sometimes I feel shame at having those emotions, making me feel even worse. Thank you for coming to earth as a human being and empathizing with the pain that can sometimes be felt on a mental level. Thank you also for modeling how we should respond to our anxiety. Give me the strength and boldness to share with people I trust about my struggle. Help me also to rely on you more—to be more dependent on you with my emotional weaknesses. Lord, be with me and be my strength.

DAY 23

Taste and See God's Goodness

Psalm 34:4-8

I sought the Lord, and he answered me and delivered me from all my fears. Those who look to him are radiant, and their faces shall never be ashamed. This poor man cried, and the Lord heard him and saved him out of all his troubles. The angel of the Lord encamps around those who fear him, and delivers them. Oh, taste and see that the Lord is good! Blessed is the man who takes refuge in him!

Think about the last time you sought God during your struggle. Whether it was good old-fashioned worry about real issues around you, an irrational anxiety consuming you, or deep sadness—think about the last time you turned to God and asked for help. Did you feel ashamed when you were done praying? Were your fears worse at the end of your prayer?

Experientially, I can say I have felt shame that kept me from praying or fears that consumed and made me think praying would not help or be worth it. I've also felt anxiety so crippling that I was physically unable to form the words of prayer.

However, whenever I was able to form a prayer, it has never hurt the situation. More often than not, I felt relief and peace in the tumultuous storm of my anxiety. More often than not, I tasted and saw it is true that the Lord is good, and I am blessed when I take refuge in Him. Therefore, I encourage you to fight to take your worries to the Lord in prayer today. I'm not saying it will be easy. I'm not saying you shouldn't take your medicine if you have a prescription (definitely not saying that). All I'm saying is that there is a real help when you can utter a cry of help to your Heavenly Father, and I implore you to do just that, no matter how far from your mind or difficult it is for you amid the storm. Please, be like David in this regard, a poor man who cried to God and received help.

Ask yourself:

When was the last time I prayed to God amid suffering? How do I typically feel after coming to God humbly with my emotional tumult?

_____

_____

_____

Why do I sometimes avoid turning to God for help when I need it most?

_____

_____

_____

Pray it back to God: Dear God, when I am overwhelmed, I don't always turn to you for help. I sometimes feel shame or feel like turning to you won't help. Heavenly Father, prove those fears wrong! Help me taste and see your comfort amid the storm. Help me to quickly turn to you and see that you are good. Thank you for your comfort, for always encamping around me and never forsaking me, even though I sometimes struggle to turn to you.

DAY 24

We Are Adopted

Romans 8:14-19

For all who are led by the Spirit of God are sons of God. For you did not receive the spirit of slavery to fall back into fear, but you have received the Spirit of adoption as sons, by whom we cry, "Abba! Father!" The Spirit himself bears witness with our spirit that we are children of God, and if children, then heirs—heirs of God and fellow heirs with Christ, provided we suffer with him in order that we may also be glorified with him. For I consider that the sufferings of this present time are not worth comparing with the glory that is to be revealed to us. For the creation waits with eager longing for the revealing of the sons of God.

We have a privilege as Christians to be called children of God and fellow heirs with Christ. However, what does this mean? Couldn't God just choose to save us from our sins and call it a day? There is great significance in being not just saved but also chosen to be adopted. You see, the wrath of God is against sin. In fact, it says in Romans 5:10, that while we were enemies of God, He saved us. We were not neutral, not ignored, but the Bible says we were enemies. When we sin, we go against God's law. I've heard it described this way: our relationship with God was like that of a criminal and the government. We broke the law and were ready for punishment, but someone paid our debt, took our punishment, and made us justified so that the government had nothing against us anymore. Being adopted means we went from being lawbreakers to having a personal relationship with God. Of course, the analogy falls short with the government and being a criminal because can you imagine being *adopted by the government*? I don't think so.

My point is, God chose not to just view us in right standing, but decided to view us as heirs with Christ, no longer a slave to fear. We can speak to our God like we speak to a loving parent. That's part of your identity. Would a good father ignore a phone call from his son or daughter when they're in trouble? No, they wouldn't. They would listen and help—that is our privilege as children of God. We are not just forgiven, but now part of a heavenly family.

Ask yourself:

Do I pray to God like I'm a part of His family?

_____

_____

_____

How should the fact that I am adopted by a good father change how I relate to God?

_____

_____

_____

Pray it back to God: Dear Heavenly Father, thank you for choosing me to adopt into your family. After all my mistakes, after all my sin, and amid my crazy mess, you chose me? Thank you for choosing and loving me. Thank you for granting me the privileges of being your child. Help me not to take that fact for granted.

DAY 25

Seek God in Distress

Psalm 18:3-6

I call upon the Lord, who is worthy to be praised, and I am saved from my enemies. The cords of death encompassed me; the torrents of destruction assailed me; the cords of Sheol entangled me; the snares of death confronted me. In my distress I called upon the Lord; to my God I cried for help. From his temple he heard my voice, and my cry to him reached his ears.

I love the word pictures used in this passage. There's a repetitive nature to the prose that really nails down the point. The psalmist uses eloquent timeless language, you may be able to relate to the 'snares of death confronting' you, or the 'cords of Sheol entangling' you (Sheol is basically another word for grave; a place of darkness that the dead go to). These phrases paint a bleak picture, but the psalmist says at the beginning that he calls "upon the Lord, *who is worthy to be praised, and I am saved from my enemies.*" He also says he calls to the Lord for help and God *hears him*. In fact, he emphasizes this by saying it in two different ways: "He heard my voice" and "my cry to him reached his ears." God really hears you when you cry to Him for help.

In 2017, I got an itchy bullseye rash on my thigh. Soon enough, I was diagnosed with Lyme Disease, and there was no telling whether I'd caught it in time. I knew a few people who were really suffering from the effects of Lyme disease. One was an older lady, and the other was a swing dancer in her 20s who had a lot of joint pain. There were so many unknowns, and I didn't know if I was destined for a life where I relied on others for care because of Lyme. Perhaps I was overreacting, and maybe I wasn't. My point is, I really felt like the cords of Sheol were entangling me. I felt so much anxiety for my future and pangs of depression as I started on the antibiotics. I turned to God in my distress, and those cords became less entangled. Yes, I still felt anxiety and fear of the unknown, but I also felt a peace that surpasses understanding. I was ready for whatever happened. You'll be happy to know that, as of now, it looks like I caught the disease early enough and it *probably* won't come back to haunt me. All I'm saying is when you feel tangled up in distress or tragedy, take it to God, and He will hear you! He may not answer the way you would like (we are not promised that), but He will hear you and have a plan for you.

Ask yourself:

What do the 'cords of Sheol entangling' look like in my context?

_____

_____

_____

Why is it essential to come to God in our distress?

_____

_____

_____

Is it enough for God to hear me, or am I only looking for Him to answer my prayer in the way I want?

_____

_____

_____

Pray it back to God: Dear God, I praise your name. When I am overwhelmed, when I feel hopeless, when it feels like I'm being placed in a coffin, hear my voice. I will seek you, and try to trust you because I know you hear me, and I know you are worthy of being praised.

DAY 26

When Your Emotions Are Tangled

Proverbs 14:13

Even in laughter the heart may ache, and the end of joy may be grief.

This is a short passage, but it's an important message. If you have experienced great suffering, you'll know that the shadows sometimes linger. This may be because of the loss of a loved one and the good times being a painful reminder that they are no longer with you. This might be because you're still discontent with your circumstances. Perhaps you've been given a great opportunity, but it's not the opportunity you want. Maybe it is simply your clinical anxiety lingering, even though your circumstances have become envious.

It's okay if you're not okay. I know it is a cheesy statement, but it's true. You don't have to dwell in shame if you don't feel the positive emotions you think you should be feeling. Maybe you are feeling guilty that your emotions are not pure and instead are muddled with the background buzz of anxiety. Whatever the case, you shouldn't beat yourself up for being a complicated person. We live in a fallen world, and even a wonderful circumstance is not truly perfect.

I think about the days leading up to publishing my first book—it had been my dream to be a published author, and there I was—anxious. People asked me, *"Are you like, BEYOND excited right now?"* and to be honest, I wasn't. I was excited, but I was also so anxious, and I felt guilty about that. Shouldn't I be jumping off the walls? Wasn't this my dream since I was little? No, it couldn't be a 'pure' emotion because the content of my first book was raw, vulnerable, and controversial. I was dealing with my idols for approval and control, so I wanted *everyone* to love the book and think I was justified in writing it. That wasn't the case, but that's okay. Publishing that book is one of the things I'm most proud of because it was a lot of work and a step of faith. I had to trust God and grow in the process. My emotions were all mixed up, and that was okay. If you find yourself with tangled-up emotions, remember that the Bible says even in laughter, your heart might be breaking, and in intense joy, you might also feel grief (Proverbs 14:13).

Ask yourself:

Do I feel ashamed for not feeling happy enough when the seasons are good?

_____

_____

_____

Do I find it hard to rejoice at the little things in a season of suffering?

_____

_____

_____

What would it look like for me to embrace the mixed-up emotions?

_____

_____

_____

Pray it back to God: Dear God, sometimes I'm a mess emotionally. At other times, I feel guilty for feeling happy and ashamed of feeling downcast if I don't think it matches my surroundings. Help me untangle my emotions and embrace multiple emotions at once. Help me see it as something affirmed in scripture and not something to feel shame for.

DAY 27

Seek Light in Darkness

Psalm 18:28-36

For it is you who light my lamp; the Lord my God lightens my darkness. For by you I can run against a troop, and by my God I can leap over a wall. This God—his way is perfect; the word of the Lord proves true; he is a shield for all those who take refuge in him. For who is God, but the Lord? And who is a rock, except our God?— the God who equipped me with strength and made my way blameless. He made my feet like the feet of a deer and set me secure on the heights. He trains my hands for war, so that my arms can bend a bow of bronze. You have given me the shield of your salvation, and your right hand supported me, and your gentleness made me great. You gave a wide place for my steps under me, and my feet did not slip.

When I am amid a rough season, I complain, cry out to God, seek help, and even fall into despair. When it's over, I often go on my way and don't stop to thank the one who helped me through that season. What an opportunity to sing praises and gratitude to my maker, savior, and sustainer, yet I choose to go about my life! I credit my own personal strength (as if!) and choose to ignore God as the one who secured my foothold on solid ground.

We are creatures designed to worship, and what a great opportunity to worship God! It is a good time to look back at difficult seasons and praise God for getting you to the other side. Yes, to praise Him, even if that season of hardship *transitioned into a new season of difficulty*. God's way is perfect. He is our rock, He is our shield, and He is our light in the darkness. He is our hope and way out of despair. I urge you to take a moment to think of times when you've been in darkness, and God got you through. Think about how hopeless you felt and how God was with you even when you didn't see Him working, He was there. Think about His goodness, praise Him for being that hope, and take courage for whatever comes.

Ask yourself:

Do I give glory to God or myself when I've made it through a difficult situation?

_____

_____

_____

What specific prayers has God answered that I've taken for granted?

_____

_____

_____

Pray it back to God: Dear God, you have indeed been my strength. It's true I've only made it through difficulties because you helped me through them. You have been with me, yet I don't always see that in hindsight. When I look back, I don't always give you praise and glory in the way you deserve. I am not capable of expressing the true praise you deserve! Yet, let me thank you now for some of the specific ways you have helped me. (Think about ways God has provided for, sustained, and protected you in the past and thank Him specifically for those times).

DAY 28

We Have Peace with God

Romans 5:1

Therefore, since we have been justified by faith, we have peace with God through our Lord Jesus Christ.

I long for peace in my innermost being. I long for my anxiety to fade into nothingness and for me to be at peace within myself. I long for my thoughts to not wage war against me, and I desire to feel accepted by the world around me instead of having an unpredictable mess of doubts, lies, and worries. If you've struggled with inner turmoil, you probably know where I'm coming from. Perhaps you long for inner peace, but I'm here to tell you (if you haven't heard me say it already) that you aren't promised inner peace in this lifetime. However, there is a better kind of peace we are gifted.

You may be at war within yourself, and your very thoughts may betray you. It may be because of our sinful natures, the influence of mental illness, or some combination of both, but if you are a Christian, God will never be at war with you. We have peace with God because Jesus justified us before God.

He paid our debts so that we can be at peace with the Father. That means even when you doubt yourself, God is remaining steadfast in His love, and being with you through it all.

In this lifetime, we may not experience what it feels like to be fully at peace within ourselves, but we can bank on peace between God and us.

Ask yourself:

Do I value the idea of inner peace more than I value my peace with God?

_____

_____

_____

How might focusing on the peace I have with God help me subsequently feel more peace within myself?

_____

_____

_____

Pray it back to God: Dear God, I want peace within myself. Help me look to a peace that is better than anything I could imagine. Help me experience peace with you and to see myself through your eyes. Help me value peace with you more than I value peace with myself.

DAY 29

We Sometimes Cling to Dust

Psalm 119:25-32

My soul clings to the dust; give me life according to your word! When I told of my ways, you answered me; teach me your statutes! Make me understand the way of your precepts, and I will meditate on your wondrous works. My soul melts away for sorrow; strengthen me according to your word! Put false ways far from me and graciously teach me your law! I have chosen the way of faithfulness; I set your rules before me. I cling to your testimonies, O Lord; let me not be put to shame! I will run in the way of your commandments when you enlarge my heart!

I love the heart posture and humility of this psalm. The psalmist is declaring the state of his heart while simultaneously praying for and reaching toward where he wants to be. He knows that life is found in God's word, yet he 'clings to the dust.' His soul melts away with sorrow, yet he asks God for the strength from His word. The psalmist is humble and knows that it's not just opening up the scriptures that will magically help him get on the right track. Therefore, he asks God to graciously teach him.

This is where our hearts should be; though we find ourselves clinging to hope in our finances, relationships, or other earthly treasures, we should acknowledge that is not the best way and ask God to help us learn. We should turn to scripture as our guide and come to God with a heart full of humility. Let us admit in the ways we fall and ask God to bridge that gap. He is the one who produces the change in our hearts when we read His word and ask Him to open our hearts.

Ask yourself:

What 'dust' do I cling to?

_____

_____

_____

Am I honest with God about how my fears and troubles are tied to things of this world?

_____

_____

_____

How can I continue to try to bridge the gap?

_____

_____

_____

Pray it back to God: Dear God, let me be honest with you, I don't always seek strength and hope in prayer or your word. I often look at things of this world, and when those things seem out of my grasp, I panic. I *grieve,* and thus, my heart reveals *that's what I'm clinging to.* Help me cling to your word. I have chosen the path you have for me. Help me walk in it. Help me delight in your words!

DAY 30

Our Future Is in God's Hands

Proverbs 27:1

Do not boast about tomorrow, for you do not know what a day may bring.

I love the Proverbs, there are so many nuggets of wisdom for your life all crowded together in one short book. This one stands out to me because I am guilty of boasting about my future, assuming I know how my life will play out. I knew I was going to be an author, didn't I? Didn't that happen? Isn't it safe to assume that I will author more books and make a substantial income from my books after many years of writing? Isn't it safe to think that my husband and I will have 3-5 kids including adoption? I'd like to count on those things, but I can't.

There's nothing wrong with planning, but the unwise part comes in when you assume you know how life will go for certain. When you look into your future for your hope and security, holding onto an idea of what is to come so tightly that you don't stop to think whether it is God's plan for you or not, you may start to resent God when that future is threatened.

I've felt these emotions and still have not fully learned my lesson. I hold my future with a slightly more open hand but still have hopes and dreams that if God chose to withhold from me, I think there would be disappointment and unrighteous anger toward God.

In the spring of 2018, I dedicated my life to Christ. After leaving a cult and wandering for years, I was finally ready, through the prompting of the Holy Spirit in my heart, to repent of my sins and believe in Jesus Christ. I remember part of that prayer being me surrendering my future to God, telling Him that whatever life He had for me, I would walk on that path. If only my hands were always as open as they were at that moment. Alas, we have sinful hearts, and our will rarely aligns with what God has planned for us! We should be aware of this and repent when withholding part of our life from the Holy Spirit's influence. When we repent of this, He is faithful to forgive us.

Ask yourself:

What future do I boast about? Am I okay with a potentially different (even radically different) future?

_____

_____

_____

Would I be angry with God if my dreams did not become a reality?

_____

_____

_____

Pray it back to God: Dear God, truly I am a sinner saved by grace. I want you to be the Lord of my life and write my story, but I know I often won't let go of the pen. There are some things I hold on to so tightly, but if they don't happen, I would like my heart to respond with acceptance of your will, although I don't know if my heart is there. Please, help me actively surrender my future to you. (Spend some time to surrender specific things to God).

DAY 31

We Have Peace not of this World

John 14:27

Peace I leave with you; my peace I give to you. Not as the world gives do I give to you. Let not your hearts be troubled, neither let them be afraid.

Our culture has distorted our idea of peace. Social media tells us that peace is being self-actualized, fulfilling your true potential, and living your life. TV says peace means having the right homeowner insurance or health insurance. You might be fooled into thinking peace means having a comma (or two) in your checking account.

Jesus offers us peace, so why are we looking for it elsewhere? The world conditions us to keep searching and grasping and reach some magical plateau to make us happy. The world teaches us that if we can get the right combination of earthly treasures and accomplishments, then we will be satisfied. When that happens, we will finally have peace. Well, guess what? The Bible points to no such plateau or magical combination. Instead, it points to Jesus as our answer for peace.

Jesus gives us the gift of peace. The more we look to Him for the answers, the more we will grow in contentment and peace. That does not mean life will get easier or storms won't come, but we have a friend in Jesus who will give us real peace. Hence, when your heart is troubled and afraid, I encourage you to look to Jesus and ask yourself if the thing making you anxious or grieved is out of His control. The answer is always no; it's never outside of His control. So please, stop seeking to reach some magical plateau of peace and look to Jesus. While some financial security, self-actualization, and good insurance might make you feel peaceful for a season, it is a false sense of safety that can't protect you.

Ask yourself:

What kind of peace do I seek? From whom or from what do I look for peace?

_____

_____

_____

How can I intentionally look to Jesus as my source of peace?

_____

_____

_____

Pray it back to God: Dear God, I want peace. I don't want to be anxious. I want lasting peace and satisfaction that does not come from anything else but you. Help me rest in your embrace and look at your character and will. Help me find lasting joy and peace despite and through my life's difficulties and emotions.

DAY 32

Fear Is Not God's Gift

2 Timothy 1:7-9

For God gave us a spirit not of fear but of power and love and self-control. Therefore do not be ashamed of the testimony about our Lord, nor of me his prisoner, but share in suffering for the gospel by the power of God, who saved us and called us to a holy calling, not because of our works but because of his own purpose and grace, which he gave us in Christ Jesus before the ages began.

God gave us the gift of the Holy Spirit, which includes all manner of spiritual richness—what it doesn't include is our fear. Our fear is not a fruit of the Spirit and should not be placed higher than the Holy Spirit. We are called to walk boldly, sharing our faith even amidst persecution. We have this calling because we've been chosen according to God's plan. We've been equipped according to God's gracious gifting to us. So, what about our fear?

We must love God and walk in step with His calling despite our anxiety or fear. This verse doesn't mean a believer is fearless, but that fear is a part of our human nature, although not part of the gifting of the Holy Spirit. Non-believers also have fear, but we have a new spirit that can walk us through even the most fearful times with love and self-control.

That line at the end, *"because of his own purpose and grace, which He gave us in Christ Jesus before the ages began"* resonates with me. It shows that God not only has a plan for us despite our sometimes very anxious hearts, but this plan has been set in motion before the world began. God knows how our whole lives will play out. Despite our failings, anxieties, depression, and weaknesses, He still chose us, forgave us, and gifted us with His Holy Spirit! So, let us walk boldly, even amid our fears, because God is with us.

Ask yourself:

Have I ever been consumed by fear?

_____

_____

_____

Why are God's gifts for me better? How can I step forward in faith despite my fears?

_____

_____

_____

Pray it back to God: Dear God, help me have boldness in my faith. Help fear not to take hold of me. Help my anxieties not to consume me. Instead, Holy Spirit give me the courage to walk in faith, no matter what may come. Help me walk intentionally in the way you've set in front of me, no matter how hard. Help me look to you for approval, strength, and refuge.

DAY 33

Don't Fear Judgment

1 John 4:17-19

By this is love perfected with us, so that we may have confidence for the day of judgment, because as he is so also are we in this world. There is no fear in love, but perfect love casts out fear. For fear has to do with punishment, and whoever fears has not been perfected in love. We love because he first loved us.

Although some biblical scholars vary in their interpretation of the end of days, the majority agree that there will be some type of "Day of Judgment". This is a day when God will judge the people of the earth, declaring some people guilty and some righteous. But dear fellow believer, you don't have to fear this judgment because in God's great love for humanity and you specifically, He made a way so that whoever believes in Him (by His divine grace) would be counted blameless. Your debt is paid because of His perfect love.

The fear of the Lord is the beginning of wisdom, but this fear does not mean fearing eternal damnation. That is off the table for you if you are a regenerate believer. What should our response be then? Our response should be to love God fully and those around us. We should also extend grace in love to those who wronged us because we've received much grace.

There may be things that overwhelm us with fear or anxiety, but our place in eternity should not be something we fear. Also, you'd do well to note that this is the most important thing and the thing you should most fear if you actually had a good reason to! I'm talking about your eternity here. If you find yourself doubting your salvation despite repenting of your sins and have asked Jesus to be the Lord of your life, those doubts you are feeling are not of God. If you are still unsure of your salvation, please reach out to a trusted fellow believer or your local pastor. You don't have to fear eternity as a believer. As someone who finds much to be anxious about, this is a sturdy rock I can be assured of. If my anxiety starts to tell me that God cannot love or forgive me, I know my anxiety is taking an irrational, absurd leap. You don't have to fear God's judgment because you have an advocate in Jesus who loves you, and that matters more than anything.

Ask yourself:

Do I fear God's wrath in judgment?

_____

_____

_____

Do I sometimes doubt God's love or forgiveness? What is the truth of scripture?

_____

_____

_____

Pray it back to God: Dear Heavenly Father, how great is your love for me! How vast is your forgiveness! Sometimes, I wonder how you could really love or forgive a sinner like me. Help me be confident in your judgment, knowing I have nothing to fear. Help me remember that you took with you on that cross everything I had to fear.

DAY 34

Joshua's Commission

Joshua 1:7-9

Only be strong and very courageous, being careful to do according to all the law that Moses my servant commanded you. Do not turn from it to the right hand or to the left, that you may have good success wherever you go. This Book of the Law shall not depart from your mouth, but you shall meditate on it day and night, so that you may be careful to do according to all that is written in it. For then you will make your way prosperous, and then you will have good success. Have I not commanded you? Be strong and courageous. Do not be frightened, and do not be dismayed, for the Lord your God is with you wherever you go."

I love this commission that God gave to Joshua. If you are familiar with the story, then you know Joshua had quite the shoes to fill when Moses died. Moses had walked in the path God had for him, including leading the people of Israel out of captivity and through the wilderness. However, because of how Moses disobeyed God's command, he could not witness the promised land that he had been leading God's people towards. Now, it was Joshua's turn to lead the people into the land, and it wouldn't be easy. After all the drama that had unfolded in the wilderness and with battles approaching, Joshua had good reason to be scared of what lay ahead. While he was being given great responsibility, God promised that if he obeyed the scripture, it would turn out well. God had made promises to the people of Israel that were going to happen. Joshua's job was to walk courageously, fight any fear He might have, obey God, and trust His promises.

God does not guarantee "good success" with all our endeavors, but He does promise to be with us, forgive us, and greet us with eternal life when this life is over. I think it's easy to take this passage out of context and stamp it on a motivational mug, "Be strong and courageous," but this isn't about managing a panic attack, being the best leader, or even about how to be a good pastor. This is a commission to Joshua from God when he's about to lead the people of Israel into God's promised land full of hardship. I want to point out the advice packed into this commission; the part about being strong and courageous is put on coffee mugs, but what about meditating on God's word day and night? What about striving to follow God's law? This is *how* you, too, can be strong and courageous. Because if you are meditating on God's law and trusting in His promises, there is nothing to fear. That doesn't mean you will never experience fear, but by reading and obeying God's word, you will find more peace. You will be able to walk confidently, knowing that you are where you need to be and God controls the outcome.

Ask yourself:

Do I meditate on God's law day and night?

_____

_____

_____

When the road is scary, do I tend to veer off?

_____

_____

_____

What is the path I should walk fearlessly in?

_____

_____

_____

Pray it back to God: Dear God, help me step up to the challenge you've set before me despite how hard or scary it may be. Help me meditate on your word day and night so that I never for a moment forget who you are and what your promises are to me. Help me not to be frightened of the life you have for me. I know I'm not promised that it will be easy, but I pray you'd be with me and help me become courageous by the power of your word.

DAY 35

Cast Your Anxieties on Him

1 Peter 5:6-11

Humble yourselves, therefore, under the mighty hand of God so that at the proper time he may exalt you, casting all your anxieties on him, because he cares for you. Be sober-minded; be watchful. Your adversary the devil prowls around like a roaring lion, seeking someone to devour. Resist him, firm in your faith, knowing that the same kinds of suffering are being experienced by your brotherhood throughout the world. And after you have suffered a little while, the God of all grace, who has called you to his eternal glory in Christ, will himself restore, confirm, strengthen, and establish you. To him be the dominion forever and ever. Amen.

I love how this passage shows us the big picture. It's so easy to get caught up in our life's busyness and everyday stresses. I don't know about you, but the more I focus on the details of scheduling, goals, deadlines, daily cleaning, that pile of laundry, and all my other recurring stressors, the more anxious I get. It's easy for me to get caught up in everything and forget what really matters. We are called to walk in obedience, striving to cast our anxieties on Him and trusting Him. We are to be watchful of pitfalls that drive us away from the peace of God.

Then when we have suffered for (did you catch this) "a little while," our God will Himself restore us, confirm, strengthen, and establish us in eternity! What an amazing promise we have!

Let us remember the big picture; let us humble ourselves and remember that we are not alone on this journey. Let us be vigilant to cut out things from our life that draw us away from God's peace. Let us be firm in our faith and share it with the world, and after a little while, it will all be worth it in eternity. Join me in casting my anxieties on God because He loves us, and knows what is best for us. I know that's easier said than done, but it's worth it every time.

Ask yourself:

Do I often forget the big picture?

_____

_____

_____

What does casting my anxieties on God look like?

_____

_____

_____

How can I remind myself of the big picture when I'm anxious?

_____

_____

_____

Pray it back to God: Dear God, I long for all this suffering to be worth it. I long for my anxiety to go away. Help me stand firm in my faith and not get caught up in the daily stresses of this life. Help me remember the life you have called me to. Help me become humble and remember that I am not the only one suffering. Keep me in your care for this "little while" of life on earth with anxiety.

DAY 36

Count Others as More Important

Philippians 2:1-4

So if there is any encouragement in Christ, any comfort from love, any participation in the Spirit, any affection and sympathy, complete my joy by being of the same mind, having the same love, being in full accord and of one mind. Do nothing from selfish ambition or conceit, but in humility count others more significant than yourselves. Let each of you look not only to his own interests, but also to the interests of others.

I love the way this passage starts, *'If there is any encouragement in Christ, any comfort from love…'* It feels almost a little passive-aggressive—not that I would put it on the apostle Paul (who wrote this letter to Philippi), but you can tell he was really trying to drive home his point. So, what is his point? Have the same love, and be in unity with one another. How does one have unity with others? This is especially hard when you consider how Christianity brings together different people.

Unity with the Christians around you means doing nothing from selfish ambition, being humble, and counting others as more important than yourself. Your anxiety might say you need to obsess over your own needs, but the Bible tells us to look at the interests of others. You'd be surprised how your anxieties start to fade when you look up from your inner turmoil and start listening to the struggles other people are dealing with. I know these scriptural commands are hard, and I'm not saying you will always be able to shift your anxiety in a moment of great distress, but I'm saying we are called to do this in general.

Ask yourself:

Am I listening to the struggles of others?

_____

_____

_____

How can I focus more on the needs of others instead of on myself?

_____

_____

_____

Pray it back to God: Dear God, help me see others as more important than myself. Help me love other people with humility and grace. Help me be quick to listen and quick to forgive. Teach me how to look out for the interests of others instead of obsessing over my own.

DAY 37

Carry Others' Burdens

Galatians 6:1-3

Brothers, if anyone is caught in any transgression, you who are spiritual should restore him in a spirit of gentleness. Keep watch on yourself, lest you too be tempted. Bear one another's burdens, and so fulfill the law of Christ. For if anyone thinks he is something, when he is nothing, he deceives himself.

If you've been in a Christian community, then the phrase, "Bear one another's burdens" might be thrown around all the time, but do you do it? Do you carry others' burdens? To those of you who are not familiar with the concept, I encourage you to obey this commandment. Over the past couple years, when I've been in stressful situations, I had people come alongside me who helped carry my burden of anxiety. I speak from experience when I say a season of anxiety *alone* is ten times harder. One of the most amazing things about the Christian community is that when we follow this command to carry each other's burdens, the burdens that fall on us in this life feel so much lighter—so much more bearable.

I implore you, don't just seek a community that can help support you in your struggle with anxiety, but start right now to carry the burdens of those around you with their unique challenges. For example, if someone loses their job, pray for them, buy them coffee, and help them with their resume. If someone loses a loved one, pray for them, let them know you are praying for them, bring food, and tell them that if they want company, you'll come over. If someone is dealing with a stressful situation with their family, (you guessed it) pray for them, ask them about the situation and be a listening ear. Also, encourage them with scripture. I know you probably didn't expect an exhortation like this in a devotional book for anxiety. However, it's crucial we don't just care for our own emotional needs but look beyond our needs to be there for our church family.

Ask yourself:

When was the last time someone helped me carry a burden?

_____

_____

How did that make me feel?

_____

_____

How can I carry the burdens of my church family?

_____

_____

Pray it back to God: Dear God, we are so self-centered, and especially when I am anxious, I can get so caught up in what I need and want that I forget other people are struggling too. Give me the strength to reach out and help others carry their burdens. Please, also bring people into my life who can help me when I'm struggling as well.

DAY 38

Pray for Each Other

James 5:16

Therefore, confess your sins to one another and pray for one another, that you may be healed. The prayer of a righteous person has great power as it is working.

I want you to read that again. Prayer changes things. Be vulnerable with your church family by sharing your sins and other struggles. If possible, find someone to meet with once a week or every other week with the specific purpose of confessing sin and praying for one another. I've made it a habit over the past few years, and it has helped my walk with the Lord. It's also helped me to be more outward-focused in a tangible way. Try to build things into your schedule that help you follow God's word.

Anxiety in itself might not be a sin, but I once heard it described as "the smoke of an idolatry fire," as we discussed early on in this devotional. Our emotions can shine a light on what's most important to us. For example, anxiety can show us just how much we value something like our approval, security, finances, or something else more than God. There may be some sinful desires bubbling under the surface that are contributing to your anxiety. Meeting with a friend for accountability will help reveal those sinful desires and turn them to God. When you meet, remind each other of the gospel and pray for each other.

When you pray for someone who's not around, why not send them a text and let them know? If you're anything like me, a text from a friend that says, *"Hey, I was just praying for you. I hope you're doing okay"* is way more meaningful to me than *"How are you doing?"*

Ask yourself:

Do I have someone in my life who I could ask to meet regularly to hold each other accountable and pray for each other?

_____

_____

_____

How can I remember to pray for my friends?

_____

_____

_____

Pray it back to God: Dear God, help me have consistent accountability and prayer in my life. Help me find someone willing to meet once a week or every other week to grow in our walk with you together. Help me consistently pray for my brothers and sisters in Christ.

DAY 39

Boast in Your Weakness

2 Corinthians 11:27-30

In toil and hardship, through many a sleepless night, in hunger and thirst, often without food, in cold and exposure. And, apart from other things, there is the daily pressure on me of my anxiety for all the churches. Who is weak, and I am not weak? Who is made to fall, and I am not indignant? If I must boast, I will boast of the things that show my weakness.

The writer of this passage was Paul, an apostle of the early church. He was a respected leader (although not at the very beginning), and he was also human. If you feel like you are somehow less than because you struggle with anxiety or have other shortcomings, let me say this very clearly: We are ALL sinners in the eyes of God who saved us by His blood. If you compare yourself to others and genuinely think your weaknesses are greater than most, take Paul's example and boast in God despite your weakness. I have anxiety, but God is faithful. I do not perform as well in my job as others, but I strive to grow so that God might be glorified through my work. I might have a fear of public speaking, but if God can use me to share my story, I will try my best to share it. So, boast in the Lord and how He can use *even you* for His glorious plans!

Be vulnerable with people. If Paul could humble himself and declare his weaknesses, then you can, too. You don't have to hide your weaknesses because when we declare our weaknesses, it makes it more evident that the good in our lives is from God. For example, I was riddled with anxiety when I wrote my memoir about growing up in a cult. The only reason I saw it through was by some divine strength provided by God to help me. He put the call on my heart so loud I couldn't ignore it, even though I didn't feel like the most emotionally equipped person. That's evidence of God showing His strength through my weakness. What about in your life?

Ask yourself:

What kind of opportunities do I have to boast about my weakness?

___

___

___

Have I been vulnerable about my struggles with trusted friends or family?

___

___

___

Pray it back to God: Dear God, help me be vulnerable with my fellow believers. Teach me how to boast about my weaknesses and see how you are using my shortcomings for a greater purpose. Give me humility that I would not try to put myself on a pedestal, but would be okay with not being perfect. Help me be content and find my satisfaction in you.

DAY 40

Don't Neglect Community

Hebrews 10:24-25

And let us consider how to stir up one another to love and good works, not neglecting to meet together, as is the habit of some, but encouraging one another, and all the more as you see the Day drawing near.

2020 was a rough year, filled with isolation, I felt this gap in friendships painfully. I know many of my friends felt it even more keenly as singles living in one-bedroom apartments. Remember back in 2020 and the pain that isolation caused? Let's strive to be a community despite quarantine. You've seen the damage to mental health in 2020 because of a pandemic and because so many of us were *alone*.

I know community can be messy and hard. I'm not saying that community is some magical cure-all. What I am saying is community can be sanctifying and a true blessing. It can be purifying because you have to learn to get along with people very different from you, and you're called to stir up one another to good works. This means you won't just be challenging others but be (ideally) you'll be challenged as well.

It's also a blessing because while you're called to encourage others, ideally, other believers will likewise be encouraging you. We need this. As creatures made in the image of God, we're created for community.

If you don't have community, seek out a church with small groups, or start a group at your own church. If you have a group, be real with them. Be vulnerable with your struggle with anxiety and be honest with your sins as well. This is something we are called to.

Ask yourself:

Do I neglect to meet with people?

_____

_____

_____

How can I be more intentional in encouraging others and holding each other accountable for the following scripture?

_____

_____

_____

How can I prioritize community?

_____

_____

_____

Pray it back to God: Dear God, I know I'm called to community, but it can be so hard. Help me go into friendships with the attitude of giving more than receiving. Help me become vulnerable in my failures and struggles. Help me encourage others even when I desperately need encouragement. Help me seek you as my source of strength and bring me blessings in my community.

DAY 41

God Is in Control

Luke 12:22-26

And he said to his disciples, "Therefore I tell you, do not be anxious about your life, what you will eat, nor about your body, what you will put on. For life is more than food, and the body more than clothing. Consider the ravens: they neither sow nor reap, they have neither storehouse nor barn, and yet God feeds them. Of how much more value are you than the birds! And which of you by being anxious can add a single hour to his span of life? If then you are not able to do as small a thing as that, why are you anxious about the rest?

Are you in control of your life? If you think yes, think again. I am a bit of a control freak, because of my sinful nature and past experiences—namely that I had little control over my life growing up—I *cling* to control. Family reunion plans get canceled last minute, then being spontaneous and making big changes all stress me out because I feel like my control is slipping away. As someone who values planning, organizing, and routines, I'm always on edge when I'm amid unpredictability. The thing is, times like that only emphasize a preexisting truth—I don't actually have control, and neither do you. Any control you perceive is just that; perceived. Did your heart skip a beat like mine did while reading what I wrote? Maybe you need to be reminded of this as much as I. We don't have control, we can't provide for ourselves, and we can't make ourselves secure.

Yet, this passage is supposed to ease our anxiety? God is the only one who can provide for us, save us, and control our lives. That scares me because I don't like letting go of my control, but the more we let go of the *illusion* of control and trust God, the more peace we will have. Why do we worry about what we should wear or when the next paycheck is coming when we literally have no control over whether we live another day? We're humans, broken, and we don't always realize God is in control, nor do we trust Him to take the wheel. Thinking we have control is like a five-year-old sitting on their parent's lap driving a car in a parking lot. The child might think they are in control, but their parent is the one who can actually reach the pedals and is the one guiding the steering wheel. As much as that five-year-old might want control and think he/she is in control, they are not in control and are ultimately safer that way.

Ask yourself:

Do I covet control? Do I start to panic when my control starts slipping away?

___

___

___

Shouldn't it be a comfort that God is in control?

___

___

___

Pray it back to God: Dear God, sometimes I'm like a kid sitting on my parent's lap with my hands on the steering wheel. I think I'm in control, and when I feel the car moving in a way I didn't intend, I start to get scared. Help me remember that you are in control, which is a *good* thing. Help me actively surrender my control to you and actually trust that you know what you are doing, even when it's impossible for me to see it at the moment.

DAY 42

The Disciples' Fear

Mark 4:36-40

And leaving the crowd, they took him with them in the boat, just as he was. And other boats were with him. And a great windstorm arose, and the waves were breaking into the boat, so that the boat was already filling. But he was in the stern, asleep on the cushion. And they woke him and said to him, "Teacher, do you not care that we are perishing?" And he awoke and rebuked the wind and said to the sea, "Peace! Be still!" And the wind ceased, and there was a great calm. He said to them, "Why are you so afraid? Have you still no faith?"

You might be tempted to think God can't use you because you don't trust Him or because your anxiety interferes with your life. Be encouraged that the people God uses are not perfect, nor are their emotions always perfect. Perhaps your anxiety is worse than the fear the disciples felt on the ship. I say "perhaps" because think about it, at this point of the disciples following Jesus, they've seen Him perform miracles. Now, here they are, amid a raging tempest, and they say to Jesus, *"Teacher, do you not care that we are perishing?"* Here are people who have Jesus, the miracle worker, in their midst, *still afraid.* If God could choose and use those trembling disciples, He can use you, too.

What do the disciples do with their fear? They go to Jesus. As Jesus points out, they have little faith, but God still moves. Think about that. God moving in your life is not dependent on whether or not you always trust Him. So, if we learn anything from this passage, let it be this: the disciples were free to go to Jesus for help, despite their level of faith.

Ask yourself:

Do I struggle thinking God could use me because of my anxiety?

_____

_____

_____

Do I think God will help me even if I have little faith at the time?

_____

_____

_____

Pray it back to God: Dear God, sometimes I have little trust in you, myself, or in your ability to use or help me. My anxiety blinds my vision. Help me grow in my faith more and more each day. Help me and use me, despite and through my anxiety.

DAY 43

Anxiety around Persecution

1 Peter 3:13-17

Now who is there to harm you if you are zealous for what is good? But even if you should suffer for righteousness' sake, you will be blessed. Have no fear of them, nor be troubled, but in your hearts honor Christ the Lord as holy, always being prepared to make a defense to anyone who asks you for a reason for the hope that is in you; yet do it with gentleness and respect, having a good conscience, so that, when you are slandered, those who revile your good behavior in Christ may be put to shame. For it is better to suffer for doing good, if that should be God's will, than for doing evil.

I can't pretend I know what all persecution feels like, especially in some parts of the world today. I've experienced persecution to a comparably *minimal* degree when I wrote my book about leaving Branhamism. When I wrote it, I received multiple emails from various old friends and relatives targeted at making me stop what I was doing. I received word of at least one sermon that was preached against me at the Branhamite churches. I also received various Facebook messages from strangers in Branhamism that said things like, *"Your book has made young people fall! You will be judged; retrace it!"* What hurt the most was my old friends and relatives making manipulative emails, even a 12-page letter, or blackmail.

Passages like this one encouraged me. I knew I was doing what God called me to and telling the truth about Branhamism and who God really is. That was what mattered, yet it didn't stop wave after wave of anxiety. It was a sanctifying time for certain. I share this with you because maybe part of God's calling in your life is going to unreached people groups with the gospel or helping at a pro-life center when your family is actively pro-choice. Perhaps part of your calling is to go to seminary school even though all your friends or family are hard-hearted atheists. Whatever your calling, if you are striving to follow Christ, you'll be persecuted at some point. When this happens, remember that the one to fear is God, and people around you have no power of ultimate judgment. God is the one in control of your life. He is the one who will hold you accountable at the end of the age.

Ask yourself:

Is the fear of what others will think or do holding me back from a call from God?

_____

_____

_____

How can I seek God's approval instead of others?

_____

_____

_____

How can I grow in trust for God amid persecution?

_____

_____

_____

Pray it back to God: Dear God, I care what people think and what they do. Help me care about what you think more than what I care about other people. I believe any evidence of that in my life is you working because I can't imagine my heart changed in such a way without your help. Give me peace in times of persecution.

DAY 44

Fearing God

Revelation 1:17-18

When I saw him, I fell at his feet as though dead. But he laid his right hand on me, saying, "Fear not, I am the first and the last, and the living one. I died, and behold I am alive forevermore, and I have the keys of Death and Hades.

In one sense, we are called to fear God, so we should care what He thinks and prioritize His law above every other authority or area in our lives. This is biblical, and it applies to us that we shouldn't fear God's eternal judgment as believers. Notice what Jesus says to John in his vision, *"Fear not, I am the first and the last, and the living one. I died, and behold I am alive forevermore, and I have the keys of Death and Hades."* What terrifying two sentences! What an awesome God we have that He would conquer death, hold the power of life and death in His hands, live on an eternal plane, and say, *"Fear not."* Yet, this is the mighty God we serve. He has all the power, and we don't have to be afraid because He *conquered death for us.*

I want you to wrestle with this idea of fearing God but not fearing His wrath. Think about what it means to be in awe of God's power and revere Him above all else while also being assured that He is for you. Imagine God, in all His majesty, speaking to you and saying what He said to John. *"Fear not..."* Meditate on this mysterious truth today.

Ask yourself:

What does it mean for me to fear (or revere) God and His word?

_____

_____

_____

What does it mean for me to be safe and secure as part of God's family?

_____

_____

_____

What should this look like in practice?

_____

_____

_____

Pray it back to God: Dear God, you are so holy and grand in majesty! Because I'm not physically witnessing your splendor, I think I forget just how terrifying you must be. Help me grow in the fear of the Lord. Help me put you first; help me hold you as the greatest priority and authority in my life. Also, help me feel safe and put away all ungodly fear, shame, or guilt. Help me feel confident in my salvation and safe when I'm in your presence.

DAY 45

Don't Fear, Only Believe

Mark 5:35-36

While he was still speaking, there came from the ruler's house some who said, "Your daughter is dead. Why trouble the Teacher any further?" But overhearing what they said, Jesus said to the ruler of the synagogue, "Do not fear, only believe."

God sees the fears of our hearts. This ruler had called Jesus to his house for Jesus to do something, but then people interrupted, saying Jesus could not help the situation; *it's too late.* This man was hearing the voices of people around him, telling him why his situation was hopeless and nothing could be done. So, Jesus told him something different. Not only was He not bothered by the ruler's request, but He told the ruler, *"Do not fear, only believe."*

Sometimes, we have people on every side telling us why the situation is helpless. Other times, those voices come from our own heads. Your anxiety might tell you the situation is hopeless; you are unloved; God does not have time for you; it's too late; you're a failure, or any number of lies that downplay the magnitude of God's love and character, or your role as a child of God. I've noticed more often than not that when God says, "Don't be afraid," it's accompanied by a mention of who He is or a reminder of a promise or something we should do. God doesn't say, "White knuckle it," "Be a man!" "Hold yourself together!" or any other toxic-coping mechanisms to deal with our fear and anxiety. Instead, He tells us to remember who He is (as in the case of Revelation 1:17-18), or He will be with us (Joshua 1:7-9), or to honor Him in our hearts (1 Peter 3:13-17), or in this case, Jesus tells the ruler to *believe*.

When your heart is troubled, and anxiety or people around you are tearing down your courage, remember to believe in God. Remember how much He loves you and just how powerful He is. Remember He sees your struggle and will always be with you. Believe in His promises, and your anxiety will start to look smaller. Then, when it feels like it's too late or God has forgotten, it's not, and He hasn't.

Ask yourself:

How can I replace my anxiety with *believing*?

_____

_____

_____

How can I ignore the voices that tear me down?

_____

_____

_____

Pray it back to God: Dear God, sometimes it feels too late. Sometimes, it feels too hard, too painful, and the voices of doubt are ringing in my ears. How can I focus on you and your promises at a time like that? God, be with me! Help me believe; though the voices in my head or people around me cause me to grow weary, hold me up with your powerful arms. Lift my head when it feels impossible to find hope. Help me see your face and believe!

DAY 46

Nothing Can Separate Us

Romans 8:37-39

No, in all these things we are more than conquerors through him who loved us. For I am sure that neither death nor life, nor angels nor rulers, nor things present nor things to come, nor powers, nor height nor depth, nor anything else in all creation, will be able to separate us from the love of God in Christ Jesus our Lord.

What can separate you from God's love? Nothing. This includes your anxiety. Don't listen to the lie that God does not love you, you are not forgiven, He can't save you, or you're not worthy. Yes, you are broken, not worthy apart from Christ's sacrifice, and you are sinful. Yes, without God, you would be utterly hopeless. However, as a believer, you're more than a conqueror, not because of what you've done but because of Him and His love for you. No one can separate you from His love or your inheritance in Christ Jesus. That's a fact.

If you feel alone, ashamed, guilty, worthless, or any other lie bombarding your mind—it does not change the fact that God loves you. Even if you might *feel* those things, it's not your reality. No matter how far your anxiety makes you spiral or what lies you find yourself believing amid a panic attack, GOD STILL LOVES YOU. You can't change that.

Death can't take it away. What's going on now can't take it away, and nothing that will happen or not happen can take it away, no matter what anyone says or does. You can rest and stay in this truth. So, the next time you hear something contrary, remember that even if you don't feel like God's love is true at this moment, it is true, and you will feel it again.

Ask yourself:

Does my anxiety ever tell me things contrary to this verse?

_____

_____

_____

How can I anchor myself in this truth even when I don't *feel* like it's true?

_____

_____

_____

Pray it back to God: Dear God, my emotions are not always truthful. My anxiety is sometimes incredibly hurtful. Please, help me remember that your word is the standard of truth, not what my anxiety might tell me. Help me feel your love tangibly, not just knowing it is there.

DAY 47

He Will Sing over You

Zephaniah 3:15-17

The Lord has taken away the judgments against you; he has cleared away your enemies. The King of Israel, the Lord, is in your midst; you shall never again fear evil. On that day it shall be said to Jerusalem: "Fear not, O Zion; let not your hands grow weak. The Lord your God is in your midst, a mighty one who will save; he will rejoice over you with gladness; he will quiet you by his love; he will exult over you with loud singing.

This prophecy was to the people of Israel, but it is also true about His attitude toward His people today. Can you imagine God singing over you? The all-powerful God of the universe taking delight in you? Psalm 147:11 says, *"But the Lord takes pleasure in those who fear him, in those who hope in his steadfast love."* It's wild to think about, but it's true. God delights in His children. As believers, Jesus has borne the weight of our failures and carried all our punishments. What is left for us? In our final judgment, our weaknesses and sins will not condemn us; instead, the Lord our God will crown us with glory and honor. He will rejoice over us! Have you ever had such good news or a good day that you just wanted to jump up and down and let everyone know? Well, God feels that way about you.

Whenever you doubt God's love for you, I want you to try and remember that. In writing these devotionals, I've mostly been just calmly writing, but today, I find happy tears in my eyes at the gravity of this truth. It would be enough that Jesus saved us from our sins, and we are forgiven—again, that *would be* enough! But praise God, He didn't stop there. He adopted us into His family.

On top of that, He gave us eternity with Him. He doesn't just love us; He *delights* over us! I find this so hard to fathom, but that's the truth of scripture. As the passage says, let our hands not grow weak, let us not fear.

Ask yourself:

Do I think of God as a wrathful, distant, or solemn God?

_____

_____

_____

What does this passage say about God's attitude toward me?

_____

_____

_____

How should this change the way I come to Him in prayer?

_____

_____

_____

Pray it back to God: Dear God, could it be true that you delight over me? Me, a sinner, a failure, a weak person? How could this be? What kind of God not just loves me but delights in me? I might never understand why you forgave me, adopted me into your family, or delighted in me. When I am anxious, I pray that you will wash over me with this truth. Truly, I'm blessed with grace and love beyond measure.

DAY 48

What Can Man Do?

Psalm 56:3-13

When I am afraid, I put my trust in you. In God, whose word I praise, in God I trust; I shall not be afraid. What can flesh do to me? All day long they injure my cause; all their thoughts are against me for evil. They stir up strife, they lurk; they watch my steps, as they have waited for my life. For their crime will they escape? In wrath cast down the peoples, O God! You have kept count of my tossings; put my tears in your bottle. Are they not in your book? Then my enemies will turn back in the day when I call. This I know, that God is for me. In God, whose word I praise, in the Lord, whose word I praise, in God I trust; I shall not be afraid. What can man do to me? I must perform my vows to you, O God; I will render thank offerings to you. For you have delivered my soul from death, yes, my feet from falling, that I may walk before God in the light of life.

I often turn to the Psalms for comfort because I can relate to David's desperate prayers to God. I want to always be learning how I can better involve God in my fight with anxiety, and what better way to learn than by reading the inspired scripture? Let's look at this passage together. This passage jumps back and forth between stating what David has to worry about, remembering who God is, and offering thanksgiving. This passage is from when the Philistines in Gath had seized David (a pretty scary time). Think about David's attitude in this Psalm. Sometimes, his prayers are more desperate and heart-wrenching, and this one isn't a walk in the park either, but his gratitude and hope stand out to me.

"What can man do to me?" He's literally been seized and is powerless, and he's asking this rhetorical question that is so full of hope. I wish this were me every time I was powerless. Oh, how I wish I could remember God's goodness and power *every time* I was worried! Alas, I'm a forgetful person in this area, and I'm guessing (since you're human) you forget this too! Let's try to learn from how David prays, being honest with God about our troubles and bearing our soul to Him while also praising His goodness and power. After all, what can man do to us? Is not the very reason you are breathing God's sustaining power at this moment?

Ask yourself:

How can I practice gratitude amid my anxiety?

_____

_____

_____

How can I be honest with God when I have doubts while declaring the ways He has come through in the past?

_____

_____

_____

Pray it back to God: Dear God, I know you see my tears and the doubts I face when I struggle. You know the storm that wages inside of me when I am anxious. Yet, you put breath in my lungs and help me wake up each new day. What can man do to me? What power does my anxiety have? You are the most powerful, wonderful, and righteous, and you are with me. I lift up your name in praise! Thank you for always being with me!

DAY 49

God Is with You in the midst of betrayal

Psalm 55:21-22

My companion stretched out his hand against his friends; he violated his covenant. His speech was smooth as butter, yet war was in his heart; his words were softer than oil, yet they were drawn swords. Cast your burden on the Lord, and he will sustain you; he will never permit the righteous to be moved.

As a king, David suffered a lot at the hands of enemies and the hands of friends. We are called into the Christian community, and we are called to love and share the gospel with those who don't know God. If we are doing those things, chances are somewhere along the way, we will feel misunderstood, or worse, attacked by someone we called a friend or family.

I know all too well what this feels like, and it's been the trigger to some scary panic attacks. That being said, though friendships have come and gone, and family members have become estranged, my God is still good. He still sustains and seeks after me, even when I sin against Him.

If part of the betrayal you have experienced is abuse, my heart is filled with empathy and compassion for you. Your Heavenly Father is unlike your earthly father, your mother, any family member, or any friend. He is always better, always loving, and always a refuge.

David was a very sinful person, not unlike the rest of us who have fallen short of the glory of God. Still, God remained with His companion. God sustained him because he was part of God's chosen people. If you ever find yourself anxious because of betrayal, remember there is someone who loves you and sticks with you even though you've betrayed Him many times. Let this overflow you with peace, love, and forgiveness.

Forgiveness doesn't necessarily mean a restored relationship, but it should mean surrendering all your fears about that relationship to God. Every time we sin against God, we are the betrayer, but we've been forgiven and welcomed into God's family. God loves us despite our betrayals, and that love should overflow into the way we handle other relationships.

Ask yourself:

Have I ever been betrayed?

Have I ever betrayed God?

How powerful is God's love for me that He would love me despite my betrayal?

Pray it back to God: Dear God, sometimes I can be distrusting of people. Help me to be quick to forgive, quick to cultivate friendships, and quick to be vulnerable. Thank you for always loving me amid betrayal, both times I've been betrayed by others and even when I have betrayed you. Help me rely on you as my most important, trusted family member and friend.

DAY 50

Peace with Community

Colossians 3:15-17

And let the peace of Christ rule in your hearts, to which indeed you were called in one body. And be thankful. Let the word of Christ dwell in you richly, teaching and admonishing one another in all wisdom, singing psalms and hymns and spiritual songs, with thankfulness in your hearts to God. And whatever you do, in word or deed, do everything in the name of the Lord Jesus, giving thanks to God the Father through him.

It's essential to lean on God amid your struggle with mental health. God is with you, and there is comfort found in His embrace. There can also be amazing comfort in community with other believers. Don't neglect meeting with other believers. Maybe you don't like the music at the churches you've tried out, or there was someone who said they'd text you but didn't, or nobody came and said hello to you…but those are not good excuses. You don't need to attend church regularly to be a Christian, but the Christian community is crucial for your spiritual growth. Not just that, it would be in direct disobedience to avoid community.

There is something about worshiping together with other believers that makes God seem bigger. It is also the same feeling about sharing answered prayers that makes us have more faith and something about a word of encouragement from a fellow struggling believer that helps you carry on. There can also be a lot of hurt despite all those amazing blessings that can come with community. Disagreements, gossiping, flaking, disappointments, and heartache can also be a part of your group of friends. People are sinful, so it will sometimes be frustrating being in a community, but we can't walk alone. Speaking from experience, cultivating a healthy community of brothers and sisters is so worthwhile, sanctifying, and brings God a lot of glory.

Ask yourself:

Does God's peace rule in my heart when dealing with other believers, or is my anxiety taking control?

_____

_____

_____

Am I in a healthy community?

_____

_____

_____

What can I do to help cultivate peace in my existing community or find a new community?

_____

_____

_____

Pray it back to God: Dear God, help me be ruled by peace. Please, surround me with people who will grow my appreciation of you. Help me feel safe to share and that people would speak the truth to me in love. Help me likewise to cultivate peace, gratitude, and encouragement in my community.

DAY 51

Sufficient for the Day Is Its Own Trouble

Matthew 6:25-34

"Therefore I tell you, do not be anxious about your life, what you will eat or what you will drink, nor about your body, what you will put on. Is not life more than food, and the body more than clothing? Look at the birds of the air: they neither sow nor reap nor gather into barns, and yet your Heavenly Father feeds them. Are you not of more value than they? And which of you by being anxious can add a single hour to his span of life? And why are you anxious about clothing? Consider the lilies of the field, how they grow: they neither toil nor spin, yet I tell you, even Solomon in all his glory was not arrayed like one of these. But if God so clothes the grass of the field, which today is alive and tomorrow is thrown into the oven, will he not much more clothe you, O you of little faith? Therefore do not be anxious, saying, 'What shall we eat?' or 'What shall we drink?' or 'What shall we wear?' For the Gentiles seek after all these things, and your heavenly Father knows that you need them all. But seek first the kingdom of God and his righteousness, and all these things will be added to you. "Therefore do not be anxious about tomorrow, for tomorrow will be anxious for itself. Sufficient for the day is its own trouble.

The passage right before this lengthy exhortation is an encouragement to us to store up treasures in heaven. I encourage you to read and meditate on the entire chapter. As is, I included so much of this passage because I think it's relevant for anyone struggling with anxiety. If you've sought scripture about anxiety before this devotional book, then no doubt you would have stumbled across this passage. I don't want you to read half-heartedly just because you've seen this passage before.

We've talked a lot about the big things in our lives that produce anxiety, but if you're anything like me, there are anxieties in the little things that sneak up daily. Things like what to wear that day, the fact that you forgot a crucial dinner ingredient, or a tiny comment your boss made that made you question your job security.

Each day, you will be faced with reasons to be anxious, but this passage urges us to consider who God is and how much He cares for us. Won't He provide for our most basic needs? Why do we worry about what we wear or what we will eat for dinner?

Ask yourself:

What small things do I obsess over?

_____

_____

_____

How can I practice making decisions without spending so much time on them?

_____

_____

_____

Do I trust God to provide for my basic needs?

_____

_____

_____

Pray it back to God: Dear God, my anxieties are sometimes focused on insignificant things like what I should wear or eat. Help me make simple decisions with peace. I've seen the ways obsessing over the little things has built up my habit of agonizing over bigger decisions or events. Help me become calm in the small things and trust your provision so that the big things can likewise not bring me as much anxiety. I know you will provide for me, but help me rest in that truth when I start to get anxious.

DAY 52

Shadow of Death

Psalm 23

The Lord is my shepherd; I shall not want. He makes me lie down in green pastures. He leads me beside still waters. He restores my soul. He leads me in paths of righteousness for his name's sake. Even though I walk through the valley of the shadow of death, I will fear no evil, for you are with me; your rod and your staff, they comfort me. You prepare a table before me in the presence of my enemies; you anoint my head with oil; my cup overflows. Surely goodness and mercy shall follow me all the days of my life, and I shall dwell in the house of the Lord forever.

This psalm is a classic for a reason. David says, *"I will fear no evil, for you are with me…"* yet he has clearly expressed fear, anxiety, and depression in other psalms. To me, him saying he 'will not fear' is a declaration of intent, a *resolution* instead of a prediction of the way he has or will handle each dark storm. In fact, I think this whole psalm is some type of resolution for himself and perhaps an exhortation to his people as well.

We know from Proverbs 27:1 that we cannot boast about tomorrow or what a new day will bring. We need to always turn to God in the dark valley and meditate on our inheritance as God's chosen people. It's unrealistic to expect to live our life in constant contentment, because we are still fallen people in a fallen world. Even so, I encourage you to reread this psalm and adopt David's words as your own resolution. We will fail in the ease with which we prioritize God and turn to Him, but that does not change the truth of who He is.

Ask yourself:

How can I take on these words as my own resolution?

_____

_____

_____

What areas are hard for me to rest in?

_____

_____

_____

Pray it back to God: Dear God, I've been trying more and more with this devotional to rest in you, but I know I'm not always going to do it perfectly, and just because I know you are my good shepherd doesn't change the fact that there will be dark valleys. Help me to not lack resolve. Let me grow in my contentment and trust for you. Refresh my soul and help me rest in the good seasons. Help me walk into your plan for me. Help me see your rod and staff when I'm walking through a valley and be comforted. Help me to always remember your promises for me.

DAY 53

Eye on the Prize

Psalm 27:1-4

The Lord is my light and my salvation; whom shall I fear? The Lord is the stronghold of my life; of whom shall I be afraid? When evildoers assail me to eat up my flesh, my adversaries and foes, it is they who stumble and fall. Though an army encamp against me, my heart shall not fear; though war arise against me, yet I will be confident. One thing have I asked of the Lord, that will I seek after: that I may dwell in the house of the Lord all the days of my life, to gaze upon the beauty of the Lord and to inquire in his temple.

Have you ever heard the expression, "Keep your eye on the prize"? Well, the concept of that expression has apparently long preceded it. David's prize is that he dwells in the house of the Lord all the days of his life. Along with the confidence that God is the most powerful and for his good, this keeps David going.

Imagine you are in a rigged boxing ring. Your outcome is set; you are going to come out of the match victorious. You will still have to fight, and those punches the other guy throws might really hurt. You might even be afraid…but why? You know you're going to get bruised up, but you also know that there is medical staff right on the other side of the ring. You know you won't lose the fight, and you know you'll be able to rest shortly, and the paycheck will be huge. Don't get me wrong, I'd be terrified in a fight like that, but our fear is often disproportionate to our situation. Our future was determined as soon as we accepted Jesus into our hearts and lives. We might get scared, but for what? The ref, medical staff, and reward are right outside the ring.

Sometimes life can get really scary whether those fears arise from potential physical harm or fears rise from our anxiety. Hence, keep your eye on the prize and remember that this whole thing is rigged. Jesus conquered sin and death so that even though you have to fight with them for a little while here on earth, you will ultimately live with your Heavenly Father in paradise.

Ask yourself:

How often do I think about "the prize"?

_____

_____

_____

When I feel anxious, do I see the battle as already won or as something I have to fight on my own?

_____

_____

_____

Pray it back to God: Dear God, help me see my struggles as temporary. Help me remember that you are with me, you have a plan for me, and I have a reward in heaven. Whom shall I fear? Thank you for winning the fight and making a way for me. Help me desire your presence more than anything else in the world.

DAY 54

Land of Silence

Psalm 94:17-19

If the Lord had not been my help, my soul would soon have lived in the land of silence. When I thought, "My foot slips," your steadfast love, O Lord, held me up. When the cares of my heart are many, your consolations cheer my soul.

Think back to when you were overwhelmed with anxiety and thought you couldn't take it anymore. Take yourself back to a moment when you were so overwhelmed that you thought you'd never get past it. Now, answer this; *how did you* get past it? Was it the passage of time, medication, calming steps your counselor taught you, a loved one talking you through it, a night's rest? Ultimately, God got you through it, even if the tool He used was the common grace of medicine, counseling, or a friend. You see, God has a steadfast love for us, a love that never waivers and will see us through to the end.

I encourage you to not run through this devotional, but instead spend time in gratitude for all the times God saved your soul from the land of silence or held you up when your anxiety weighed heavily upon you. Let His consolations cheer your soul; bask in His steadfast love. If you have to leave for work in a moment or have a young child tugging on your shirt and asking for breakfast, I encourage you to find moments in the day when you can meditate on the ways He's shown you steadfast love. A few moments of gratitude will be worth it in the mundane or chaos of your day.

Ask yourself:

What times has God saved me from my anxiety?

_____

_____

_____

How did I get past it when I was at a breaking point?

_____

_____

_____

How has God's steadfast love been evident lately?

_____

_____

_____

Pray it back to God: Dear God, you have been with me in every anxious moment. You were there to hold me up through every struggle, grief, or fall. Your steadfast love keeps me from staying down. You love me in every moment and help me continue. Thank you for consoling me and bringing cheer to my soul when anxiety feels like it will never leave. Thank you for all those times in the past and the ways I know you will rescue me in the future.

DAY 55

Remember What God Has Done

Psalm 77:4-13

You hold my eyelids open; I am so troubled that I cannot speak. I consider the days of old, the years long ago. I said, "Let me remember my song in the night; let me meditate in my heart." Then my spirit made a diligent search: "Will the Lord spurn forever, and never again be favorable? Has his steadfast love forever ceased? Are his promises at an end for all time? Has God forgotten to be gracious? Has he in anger shut up his compassion?" Selah Then I said, "I will appeal to this, to the years of the right hand of the Most High." I will remember the deeds of the Lord; yes, I will remember your wonders of old. I will ponder all your work, and meditate on your mighty deeds. Your way, O God, is holy. What god is great like our God?

Have you ever been so troubled that you couldn't speak? We've all had great sorrow in our lives. For me, that sorrow was seeing people I love being abused. It was being molested as a child, sexually harassed as an adult, and losing all my friends when I left Branhamism. But no matter what your great sorrows look like, do not think God has forgotten you or His steadfast love has ceased.

If you have the time to read the entire psalm, I encourage you to read it from start to finish. This psalm starts with the psalmist saying his soul refuses to be comforted and ends with a list of all God has done for the people of Israel. Finally, the psalmist lays out all the big things He knows God has done for His people, which prove His steadfast love and that He keeps His promises.

For some of us, it is all too easy to meditate on the great sorrows of our past, but I urge you to look into your past, and scripture, and meditate on all the good God has done. What promises did He make to you through scripture that He has not fulfilled? What time of your life has He not been ready with forgiveness after sin, and what time of your life was He not present with you despite a sorrowful time? The past does not just hold sorrow; looking into the past can also shine a light on the goodness of God's character. God is faithful to extend grace and fulfill His promises despite what our anxious thoughts might say.

Ask yourself:

When I look into my past, does it bring me sorrow?

_____

_____

_____

How does that past change if I focus more on what God has done instead of looking at the tragedies, regrets, and losses?

_____

_____

_____

Is God faithful?

_____

_____

_____

Pray it back to God: Dear God, sometimes I've felt so troubled that even speaking is hard. You know my heart, God! You know me, and you know everything I've been through. I pray you would redeem my past and help me see the ways you were with me and worked for my good. Help me take comfort in your faithfulness all throughout scripture to keep your promises. Help me see what you are doing in my broken story, even if only in part.

DAY 56

Dwelling in Safety

Psalm 4:6-8

There are many who say, "Who will show us some good? Lift up the light of your face upon us, O Lord!" You have put more joy in my heart than they have when their grain and wine abound. In peace I will both lie down and sleep; for you alone, O Lord, make me dwell in safety.

Think about the celebrity or a successful person that you most admire. Now, imagine you were walking a day in their shoes. Do you think that would make you genuinely happy or peaceful? Our heroes can sometimes be a wake-up call to the emptiness of the things we desire.

A couple of years ago, I was in tears when a New York Times best-selling author I admired announced that she was going through a divorce. Here was someone who had so much of the things I aspire to, yet her life was falling apart in other ways. Whether or not I wanted to admit it, part of me said if I could just get *there*, I would be satisfied, safe, and secure. Unfortunately, we cannot find our joy and peace from money, fame, relationships, accomplishments, or *anything else apart from*

God. The joy and peace that God provides are better than any temporary joy we might find in having a lot of 'grain and wine.'

The only thing we can be secure in is our God's love for us. He will sustain us; He will make us lie in safety, and by His grace, He will enable us to rise the next day. Whether you have plenty of good in your life or feel like the world is crumbling around you, look upon the face of the only one who can bring you peace.

Ask yourself:

Who do I idolize or envy?

_____

_____

_____

Will my greatest desire bring me joy apart from God?

_____

_____

_____

Pray it back to God: Dear God, help me grow in contentment and be secure in my identity as someone loved by you. When I lay my head down to rest tonight, help my sleep be peaceful, knowing that you alone make me dwell in safety. Remind me that security sought apart from you is not true security.

DAY 57

God Has a Place for You

John 14:1-3

Let not your hearts be troubled. Believe in God; believe also in me. In my Father's house are many rooms. If it were not so, would I have told you that I go to prepare a place for you? And if I go and prepare a place for you, I will come again and will take you to myself, that where I am you may be also.

I must remind myself that this is not our home, and God wants us to live with Him. Jesus spoke these words to His disciples after He had been sharing about His upcoming death and resurrection. His disciples were (understandably) confused and distressed at what He had been sharing, which is how He encouraged them.

Believer, if you are struggling to find peace amid your anxiety and this crazy world, there is comfort to be found in the fact that your anxiety and the chaos you see around you *will not* be forever. When you get caught up in planning what you will eat, where you will live, or what you will do in the next five years, take comfort in knowing that the best planner ever to exist is in charge of your eternity plans. He knows where you will live here on earth and in heaven. I hope the knowledge God has prepared a place for you fills you with more security and peace than a sturdy retirement plan ever could.

Ask yourself:

Do I believe God wants to live with me?

_____

_____

_____

Do I find comfort in the fact that God has prepared a place for me in heaven?

_____

_____

_____

Pray it back to God: Dear God, help me remember when I'm distressed and confused about my future that you are the ultimate planner, and you have my life planned out all the way into eternity. Help me trust your plans and remember you are not just with me now, but you desire to spend eternity with me.

DAY 58

Remember His Steadfast Love

Psalm 31:1-5 & 21-22

In you, O Lord, do I take refuge; let me never be put to shame; in your righteousness deliver me! Incline your ear to me; rescue me speedily! Be a rock of refuge for me, a strong fortress to save me! For you are my rock and my fortress; and for your name's sake you lead me and guide me; you take me out of the net they have hidden for me, for you are my refuge. Into your hand I commit my spirit; you have redeemed me, O Lord, faithful God. (...) Blessed be the Lord, for he has wondrously shown his steadfast love to me when I was in a besieged city. I had said in my alarm, "I am cut off from your sight." But you heard the voice of my pleas for mercy when I cried to you for help.

In this psalm, David pleads for help and declares the truth that God is with you when you are in. He is faithful to fulfill His promises and show you His steadfast love. Don't be afraid to ask boldly for Him to "rescue you speedily." God delights in the prayers of His children, and He loves it when you depend on Him. When you think you are "cut off from God's sight," think again. God hears your cries for help and sees each of your tears.

Romans 8:26-27 says, "Likewise the Spirit helps us in our weakness. For we do not know what to pray for as we ought, but the Spirit himself intercedes for us with groanings too deep for words. And he who searches hearts knows what is the mind of the Spirit, because the Spirit intercedes for the saints according to the will of God." Even if you cannot voice the words aloud, let your spirit and thoughts raise a voice to the heavens because God knows your thoughts. He will always have steadfast love for you, no matter what you do or how you feel. It is never too late for God to rescue you and reveal to you His steadfast love.

Ask yourself:

How many times have I thought God was too late, but He showed up anyway?

_____

_____

_____

Shouldn't I think back to the evidence of God's love for me?

_____

_____

_____

Is His love not steadfast?

_____

_____

_____

Pray it back to God: Dear God, help me remember your steadfast love. Be my rock for me to stand on and my refuge from the storm. May your promises always anchor me, oh God! You have redeemed me from a purposeless life into your glorious presence and purpose! When I feel like I am all alone, I know that's not true. You are always with me. Thank you for your steadfast love; help me to always remember.

DAY 59

Flooding with Tears

Psalm 6:1-10

O Lord, rebuke me not in your anger, nor discipline me in your wrath. Be gracious to me, O Lord, for I am languishing; heal me, O Lord, for my bones are troubled. My soul also is greatly troubled. But you, O Lord—how long? Turn, O Lord, deliver my life; save me for the sake of your steadfast love. For in death there is no remembrance of you; in Sheol who will give you praise? I am weary with my moaning; every night I flood my bed with tears; I drench my couch with my weeping. My eye wastes away because of grief; it grows weak because of all my foes. Depart from me, all you workers of evil, for the Lord has heard the sound of my weeping. The Lord has heard my plea; the Lord accepts my prayer. All my enemies shall be ashamed and greatly troubled; they shall turn back and be put to shame in a moment.

The Lord sees us when we "flood our bed with tears," have a panic attack, or have an all-around anxious day. He sees us and hears our pleas for help. So, let's learn from David, to be honest with God and to turn to God amidst grief, heartache, and fear. If you are growing weary, tell God. Of course, He knows what you are going through and has a compassionate heart for you, but when we share with God our hearts, we exercise our trust for Him. It's one thing to know God sees your heart and another to be vulnerable and declare your need for Him.

God not only sees us, but He hears us when we cry out to Him. He hears our prayer and accepts it. As a result, our worries will flee from us, and our anxieties will fade away. That might not be in a moment, but we know God shows up in amazing and often unexpected ways when His children cry out to Him.

Ask yourself:

Do I plead with God?

_____

_____

_____

Am I honest with Him about my emotions?

_____

_____

_____

Pray it back to God: Dear God, help me become honest with my emotions and what is going on in my life. I sometimes take for granted that you already know and I neglect to share my heart with you. Lately, I have felt...(share how you've been doing lately concerning your struggle with anxiety or other things that have been hard for you). I am so needy, God, so in need of you. I don't want to pretend I have it all together when I pray to you. I want to be honest about my struggles and see you meet me where I am and comfort me.

DAY 60

Refuge and Strength

Psalm 46:1-7

God is our refuge and strength, a very present help in trouble. Therefore we will not fear though the earth gives way, though the mountains be moved into the heart of the sea, though its waters roar and foam, though the mountains tremble at its swelling. Selah There is a river whose streams make glad the city of God, the holy habitation of the Most High. God is in the midst of her; she shall not be moved; God will help her when morning dawns. The nations rage, the kingdoms totter; he utters his voice, the earth melts. The Lord of hosts is with us; the God of Jacob is our fortress.

This might be the last day of this devotional, but it shouldn't be the end of you getting into God's word and talking to God regularly. Regularly reading scripture and meditating on the passages that contradicted my anxiety's lies has helped me so much in my fight against anxiety. God is our refuge, strength, and the very present help when we are struggling.

Though the earth gives way, your future with God is determined. The next day will come and then the next until we finally see our Heavenly Father in His heavenly kingdom. That is what we have to look forward to: a world where there are no more anxious or troubled heart. Until then, we know God has a plan for us as unique sons or daughters.

We must keep leaning on God and trusting Him despite and through our anxiety. When things come that usually worry us, let us be a people quick to pray instead of turning immediately to fear. When we can't stop the fear, let us be courageous, knowing God is with us. He is our strength, and He cares for us. My hopes and prayers for this book are that you will continue to fight the lies your anxiety attacks you with and find joy and peace in the promises and comfort of our Heavenly Father.

Ask yourself:

What has been my biggest takeaway from this devotional book?

_____

_____

_____

Which verses helped me the most?

_____

_____

_____

How can I continue to study and meditate on those verses?

_____

_____

_____

Pray it back to God: Dear God, I know my struggle with anxiety does not end with reading a devotional book. Help me trust you despite and through all my anxieties. Help me remember who I am, who you are, and your promises to me. Help me become courageous and have peace that only you can give. Help me live out the purposes you've created me for, even when I have anxiety. In Jesus Christ's name I pray, Amen.

CLOSING COMMENTS

Reading your Bible or praying is not a substitute for professional help. Neither is professional help a substitute for spending time in seeking comfort from your Heavenly Father. I will always encourage both.

If your anxiety impairs your ability to function or becomes overwhelming, ask for help. There should be no shame in taking medication, going to counseling or therapy, or spending time in recovery.

Talk to your primary health care provider to see if you need to start or change any medications.

Be vulnerable with trusted family members or friends. You not only have a Heavenly Father who loves you but other people too. If you don't know who to turn to, consider talking to someone on staff at your local church.

More people suffer from anxiety than you might think. As you share your struggle, you may find other people who have gone through or are currently going through the same things.

Identify recurring toxic thoughts, and when you are able to, seek out scripture that is saturated with truth. Meditate on these scriptures, put them on your mirror, or work with an app to memorize them. This practice has helped me when the lies start to spitfire in my head, because I have something to help ground me and fight those thoughts.

Practice praying a simple prayer when you are not anxious; something like "Jesus be with me," or "Help me through this," or "Give me wisdom." Then when you are anxious, your practice will aid as a kind of muscle memory to help you be able to form the words of the prayer, whether in your head or out loud.

Remember, you are not alone. You are a loved individual who was made in God's image. If you are a believer in Christ, you can be assured that you are a child of God, adopted into His family. You have a family in God and believers around you. God has a plan for you, and He will be with you to see it through. When the toiling ends and you meet God face to face, it will all be worth it, and we will see what the fullness of joy feels like. Until then, let us seek to love God with all our soul, mind, and strength, despite and through our anxiety.

RESOURCE LIST

If you are interested in learning more about mental health from a biblical perspective, I recommend the books below.

1. *Grace for the Afflicted: A Clinical and Biblical Perspective on Mental Illness* by Matthew S. Stanford
2. *Troubled Minds: Mental Illness and the Church's Mission* by Amy Simpson
3. *Untangling Emotions: God's Gift of Emotions* by J. Alasdair Groves
4. *Why Do Christians Shoot Their Wounded?: Helping (Not Hurting) Those with Emotional Difficulties* by Dwight L. Carlson

www.ingramcontent.com/pod-product-compliance
Lightning Source LLC
Chambersburg PA
CBHW070849050426
42453CB00012B/2112